THE
BECKY
C O D E
Don't Waste Your *magic*

How to Deal With White Woman Violence While Amplifying Your Joy!

Catrice M. Jackson, MS, LMHP, LPC

International Best Selling Author

Published by Catriceology Enterprises Omaha, NE | United States of America

FOR INFORMATION CONTACT: Catrice M. Jackson, M.S., LMHP, LPC, Global Visionary Leader of the Awakened Conscious Shift, International Speaker and International Best-Selling Author

Online ordering is available for all products. www.thebeckycode.com www.catriceology.com and www.shetalkswetalk.com

ISBN-13: 978-0983839859 (Catriceology Enterprises) ISBN-10: 0983839859

Book Cover Design: Ozone Media Group

Editor: Marian L. Gallagher

Interior Design: Jennifer Turner

Printed in the USA 10 9 8 7 6 5 4 3 2

THE

BECKY

CODE

Don't Waste Your Magic

Table of Contents
Becky Decoded

Dedication

"In a world that directly and indirectly tells Women of Color they are not worthy, qualified, invited, beautiful, or valued, we must deny EVERY restriction, affliction, prediction, and depiction that causes us to stay captive, be unhealed, doubt our destiny, and fail to embrace our beauty."

– Catrice M. Jackson

This book is dedicated to you, to every black, brown, Native. and Indigenous woman alive, and to those who came before you. Women of color have endured some of the most horrific, tragic, and despicable acts of violence committed against them for centuries, and still you keep resisting and rising. White women try to suffocate you, but they don't know how resilient your roots are. They don't know how glorious you are. They don't know that you are the heir of greatness! They don't know the power of your melanin magic!

Black, brown, Native, and Indigenous women have been resisting oppression and persisting long before white women hopped on the bandwagon. We are the original leaders of the women's movement. It's time to take your rightful place. It's time for you to take back your power. It's time for you to lead again. I wrote this book for YOU, my Sister. This is your guide. This is your little black book for winning the battle of Becky. This one is for you. Now go forth, and activate your magic, and amplify your joy! Be unwavering. Be unapologetic. Be unstoppable! You've got this. I've got you. We've got each other and we WILL win!

Preface

As soon as you open your eyes each morning, *it* begins. *It* is a fierce game of mental gymnastics that you engage in to prepare yourself for navigating a hostile world. Perhaps you dread another day of walking on eggshells, tiptoeing through social land mines, and holding your breath while trying to survive, all while proving your worth. Every damn day you must go to greater lengths than white women to be seen, heard, valued, and believed. Why? Because you exquisitely and phenomenally exist in your beautiful black or brown skin.

It's rare that a day goes by in which you are not required to modify your behavior, minimize your presence, and/or make sacrificial accommodations in order to keep white folks emotionally comfortable. You've had to learn how to shift, shuffle, and stay silent as a means of long-term survival. In all your gloriousness, your greatness will always be questioned in a society that prefers and caters to whiteness. And there's a particular kind of Whiteness that causes serious harm to your mental, emotional, and spiritual well-being: the whiteness you'll experience from every white woman. And this white woman's name is Becky.

Beckys will claim they are your sisters in the fight for equality, while championing their causes with their feet on your back. And when you complain about the pain they cause you, they'll deny they're standing on you. They'll tell you to stop complaining, and to stop creating your *own* problems. I know you've been dealing with Becky's wrath for a long time, and it's exhausting. I know that white women silence, violate, and oppress you in many ways, and it's taking a toll on you. I know that these episodes with Becky can cause you to feel paralyzed, angry, sad, and confused. Sister, I also *know* that Becky gets on your last damn nerve!

And when you allow Becky and her Beckery to zap the life from you and exhaust you, she vaporizes your precious life source. She fractures the essence of your gloriousness! She steals your joy, and Sister, you can't thrive without joy. I wrote this book because black, brown, Native, and Indigenous women like you have been suffering from White Woman Violence since forever. And often times, we've been suffering in silence. Many women of color *know* this violence is happening to them, but they don't know what to call it, how to address it, and/or how to prevent it from overwhelming them. Is it happening to you? Are you being violated and exhausted by the Beckery? I wrote this book for you, Sister.

The Becky Code shares a message I've been carrying with me for a lifetime. This is a long overdue message that clearly identifies what White Woman Violence is and how Becky harms you with her Weapons of Whiteness. You don't have to try to decipher this Beckery on your own. I have decoded Becky, her motives, and her tactics, and I offer you *Weapons for Winning* to use when Becky comes at you with her violence. Nah! I need you to refuse to let Becky win! I know you're sick and tired of dealing with Becky and her Beckery! She isn't going anywhere, so you must learn how to DEFY her Beckyism.

The Becky Code meticulously deconstructs Becky to reveal the Weapons of Whiteness she uses to silence, marginalize, harm, and oppress Women of Color. Becky is exhausting. Don't waste your magic on her! You're not MAGIC for nothing! Yes, Girlfriend, when Becky comes to Deny, Defend, Derail, and Destroy, you can whip out the *Four D's for Defying the Beckery* to defy her Beckery. You can use these Weapons for Winning to deflect her destruction, protect your power, and amplify your JOY! *The Becky Code* teaches you how to defy her deadly weapons, resist her wrath, and activate your magic to not only survive, but to thrive, and to experience deep, rich, and abundant joy!

Introduction

Who is Becky?

Have you ever met a white woman who didn't emotionally exhaust you and literally suck the life out of you? What about a white woman who did not silence, violate, or oppress you? How about a white woman who did not center herself, her feelings, and her issues in a conversation? And finally, have you ever engaged with a white woman that did not become defensive, emotionally fragile, and/or jump into fight-or-flight mode when discussing racism? If you're like most women of color, the answer is no. Why do white women show up this way when engaging with black, brown, Native, and Indigenous women? Were they taught these behaviors, and by whom? Is there a *secret* script for white women that you don't know about? What the hell is going on with white women?

White women are psychologically violent and exhausting! They will literally vaporize your emotional energy if you do not protect it. This is Becky and her Beckyism. *Beckyism* is the violent and oppressive way in which white women who are not doing any personal anti-racism work will engage with women of color. As a result of white supremacy and white privilege, white women believe they can say and do anything they want when engaging with black, brown, Native, and Indigenous women without suffering any consequences. Beckyism is dismissive, accusatory, and oppressive, and Becky works to violate, silence, and marginalize women of color. This is what white women do to black, brown, Native, and Indigenous women all the time. This is what Becky does. The emotionally abusive behaviors I describe above are toxic to your well-being, and they are what I call Beckery!

Beckery is the oblivious, obnoxious, and oppressive way in which white women view the world through their white supremacist lenses that leads to invalidating, insulting, and assaulting people (especially women) of color with violent Weapons of Whiteness. Beckery is intentional, insidious, and invasive. Some Beckys know exactly what they're doing, while others act out of willful ignorance on the daily. Both ways of showing up invade your space, peace, and joy. Beckery aims to do one of four things to people of color and their lived racial experiences:

Deny, Defend, Derail, and Destroy.

Sister-friend… Sister-friend…

Phew!

Becky…Becky…BECKY!

I know you *know* Becky, and if you don', maybe the following descriptions will sound familiar to you. Have you ever engaged with any of these Beckys?

- **Super Becky:** A savior-complex Becky who is notorious for jumping into conversations about racism to Save-A-Black or Brown woman without their consent.

- **Begging Becky:** A performative Becky who is always sniffing around, panting for pats on the back, and begging for Ally Cookies (accolades and praise).

- **Wanna-Be-Black Becky:** A Becky who loves to date black men/women, fetishizes black women, and appropriates AAVE to appear "woke."

- **Talk-Too-Damn-Much Becky:** A talkative, centering Becky who adds no value, validity, or validation in race talks.

- **Know-It-All Becky:** A condescending, apathetic Becky who intellectualizes racism by using a cognitive approach to understanding and discussing racism.

- **Love-and-Light Becky:** An oblivious Becky who selfishly uses a sprinkling of love, light, and woo-woo talk to avoid facing her racism and to minimize your oppression.

- **Whining-Ass Becky:** The most fragile Becky of all. She's perpetually hurt about anything and everything related to racism. She's a master at crying a river of White Tears.

- **Ole-Thieving-Ass Becky:** A Becky who rapes and robs the culture of black and brown people to create an identity so she can feel alive inside.

- **Get-On-Your-Nerves Becky:** A Becky who just gets on your nerves. She's a combination of Talk-Too-Damn-Much Becky and Know-It-All Becky, and she will exhaust the hell out of you.

- **Coworker Becky:** A Becky who smiles in your face and tries to sabotage your success at work.

- **BWAM (But What About Me?) Becky:** A Becky whose favorite Weapon of Whiteness is Centering. She becomes fragile and defensive when she's not getting all of the attention.

I told you that you *know* Becky! What you've read is just a glimpse of the *Beckery* in Becky's weaponry that I call *White Woman Violence*. She is armed and dangerous with deceptive and harmful behaviors known as *Weapons of Whiteness*.

The Becky Code is your guide for dealing with White Woman Violence. I describe these Weapons of Whiteness in detail and provide tangible and nourishing strategies to defy the Beckery and to preserve your precious emotional energy, and I also offer tips on how to amplify your joy. In this book, you'll learn why and how white women use Weapons of Whiteness against you by first examining the legacy of White Woman Violence and its toxicity. You'll then gain greater insight into Becky's Beckery and the emotional violence she inflicts upon you, and you'll finally be able to name her violence and call it out for what it is.

I've spent a lot of years analyzing Becky, trying to figure out why she interacts with women of color the way she does, and I have cracked the Becky code for you. Becky's mindset is meticulously broken down so you can understand the *Beckyology* of white women and why they're violent toward you. It's essential that you understand her motives, intentions, and behaviors because she is trying to sink you into a very dark place that I refer to as the *Sunken Place*. And I know you've been there before. When Becky comes for you, it can literally suck the life out of you and create a tremendous amount of anger, sadness, and pain.

Becky is trying to steal your life source. She's trying to steal your joy. I refuse to let white women win this way, which is one reason I wrote this book. Sister-friend, you do not have to put up with Becky's White Woman Violence.

- You, my Sister, are magical!

- You are glorious and magnificent.

- You exist as greatness already, and you are here to fulfill your destiny!

- You have a special purpose for living, and if you let Becky suck the life out of you, not only does *she* win yet again, you *lose* the light and fire within.

I know you're tired of dealing with Becky, but get ready to revitalize your life with the codes for defying Becky and her Beckery. The best way to defy Becky is to know her, and *The Becky Code* gives you the insights you need to deal with her violence while amplifying your joy!

Are you ready to crack this code and say, "Nah, not today, Becky!"

Yes, my Sister, it's time for you to win the Battle of Becky!

Go forth, Sis… and WIN!

The Risk of Befriending the Rose

By Catrice M. Jackson

I don't *know* if it's possible. It's certainly not necessary.

But I can tell you what it feels like.

Slow… insidious…antagonizing. Often psychologically torturous.

An exhausting emotional death, by a thousand paper cuts.

Tiny yet painful cuts. Sometimes invisible, but they hurt like hell!

Why do we continue to attempt to hold the Rose, with thorns?

When we KNOW it will prick us, stick us, and cause us to bleed?

We see the beauty in the Rose. We want to bring it near us.

Yet we know it hurts us.

Often we admire the Rose from a distance, because we just can't take another "accidental or unintentional" prick or poke.

We reach for it, and then quickly draw back, because we KNOW it was created to poke, pinch, and slice our skin with tiny, yet painful cuts.

We know it will draw blood.

Some of us say "Screw it" and choose to never reach for the Rose.

Some of us continue to keep our distance from the Rose.

While others try to figure out how to hold the Rose as close as possible without getting wounded.

I don't *know* if it's possible. It's certainly not necessary.

The Rose was born with thorns and to hold it means to risk getting cut.

The Rose.

Often deemed the most revered and desirable flower

doesn't matter what shade the petals are. They all have thorns. It's unavoidable.

Some people say, "Leave them damn roses alone!"

Often, I agree and I do.

The Rose has a name.

She is a White Woman.

To befriend her, to hold her, is to know that blood will be drawn.

She was created with thorns.

Thorns of unconscious, biased beliefs.

Thorns of implicit, racist thoughts.

Thorns of intentional and unintentional psychological attacks.

She cuts with…

denial, blame, justification, and minimization.

She slices your soul with

rationalization and defensiveness.

Microaggressions.

Invalidation.

Racial superiority.

And when you finally have had enough trauma…

She cries.

She runs.

She hides.

She's hurt, and she's offended that you would have the audacity to point out and complain about her thorns, all while denying that the thorns even exist.

She's fragile.

You see them.

You've felt them.

You *know* they're there.

And if you dare attempt to help her see her thorns, she lashes out.

She cuts and cuts. Slices, and slices, and her thorns speak…

I'm not racist. I have black friends.

I'm not racist. I'm married to a black man.

I'm not racist. My children are half black.

I'm not racist. My neighbors are black.

I'm not racist. My brother's wife is black.

I'm not racist. We have black people in our family.

I'm not racist. I work with black people and love them.

I'm not racist. I do not see color.

I'm not racist. I think people are people. We're all human.

Every thorn cuts.

She draws blood

she wounds.

And every time you reach for her, every time you attempt to hold her, you *know* you will be cut.

It doesn't matter what shade the petals are. She was born with thorns.

And to continue to attempt to hold her,

you agree to death by a thousand paper cuts. Because racism is trauma.

You agree to participate in the cycle of violence.

You know… the invisible, imminent cycle of violence that many women find themselves in with abusive partners?

The cycle when the relationship begins in the honeymoon phase. Where you laugh, and you talk, and you smile. You do lunch, you engage. It feels good.

You begin to think you can actually have a relationship with the Rose. Until the day…

you step out of place.

Until the day… you speak truth.

Until the day… you call out the reality of *your* truth.

Until the day… you begin to deeply talk about race, racism, and white supremacy.

On THIS day, in THIS moment, you move into the next phase of the cycle of violence.

She distances herself.

She's quiet.

She's silent.

She's fragile.

She's hurt.

She's now angry!

She lashes out…

She accuses YOU of being the one with the problem. She accuses YOU of being the one who is starting trouble. She accuses YOU of being the one who is racist.

Punch.

Slap.

Kick.

Your "friend" just attacked and assaulted you. What the hell just happened?

Emotional abuse. At its best.

Sometimes you take it and stay,

sometimes you know your worth and you walk away,

Sometimes you fight back and become overwhelmed with Racial Battle Fatigue.

Most times you leave and never come back. *Because you've been here before.*

If your relationship is slightly beyond superficial, she'll apologize. She'll say she's sorry. She'll ask for your forgiveness.

But not without… some justification, some minimization, some rationalization, and White Fragility galore!

If you forgive her, you willingly move into the next phase of the cycle of violence.

You walk on egg shells, wondering *when*, not if, it will happen again.

It usually does. You see, she was born with thorns. She was created to cut.

I don't know if it's possible.

It's certainly not necessary.

But I can tell you *this*! To befriend her is to experience...

Slow… insidious…antagonizing emotional death.

Death by a thousand paper cuts.

Tiny yet painful cuts that hurt like hell.

So, what happens now?

There are only three options.

Reach for the colorful tulips and daisies instead.

Leave them damn roses alone.

Or, she chooses to remove her thorns.

Yet a Rose… is not a Rose… without her thorns. She will always be a Rose.

8 Reasons Women of Color Don't Trust White Women

Sister-friend, I know you don't trust Becky, and your reasons for not trusting her are completely legitimate. The following are eight common reasons why women of color do not trust white women. These are the toxic roots of Becky, Beckery, and her Beckyism.

- Collectively white women don't give a damn about women of color.

- White women notoriously use Weapons of Whiteness to assault women of color.

- When white women claim they are colorblind you know they are lying.

- White women love to silence women of color.

- All white women are racist.

- White women's thirst for attention marginalizes women of color.

- White Feminism is toxic and lethal.

- White women have been colluding with white supremacy for centuries

"Hate is too **great** a *burden* **to bear.** It injures the **hater** more than it injures the **hated**. **"**

-Coretta Scott King

CHAPTER ONE
The legacy **of**
White Woman **Violence**

"White women have **mastered** the art of weaponizing their Whiteness. It's dangerous and deadly." – Catrice M. Jackson

---

"Sell her, sell her, sell the Negress!" Says Mistress Epps screams the words at her husband. Mistress Epps who is sick and tired of her white, plantation-owning husband shamelessly lusting after Patsey, a black slave woman subjugated to Master Epps' on-demand sexual assaults. Mistress Epps, the woman of the house on the Epps Plantation, vehemently aware that her husband, the Slave Master, is sadistically fond of Patsey, one of his favorite slaves. Mistress Epps, disgusted, envious, and violently vocal with diabolical disdain for Patsey, demands that she be sold like livestock.

White women have been violent towards black women since our first interactions with them. Refusing to acknowledge our humanity or to treat us as human, they've never been our sisters. Mistress Epps, the Antagonist in the movie 12 Years a Slave, perfectly depicts the roots of the White Woman Violence we experience in real life today.

> The movie 12 Years a Slave is an adaptation of a true story based on the autobiography of Solomon Northup. The book 12 Years a Slave was published in 1853 and sets a horrific scene, one that illustrates the legacy of White Woman Violence still alive and thriving in present-day America. Solomon Northup, an African-American born free in New York City, is kidnapped in Washington D.C. and sold into slavery in 1841. From 1841 to 1853, Solomon endured twelve years of brutality, degradation, suffering, and immense grief as a slave in the Deep South. Two things helped him get through his ordeal; his desperate belief that he would one day be free and see his family again, and Patsey, a slave woman who offered him a glimmer of joy during the long and treacherous years of captivity. In this chapter, I share two significant scenes so you can experience the deadly dialogue that illustrates White Woman Violence. Both scenes take place in Avoyelles Parish, in a small town near Bunkie, Louisiana at the Epps Plantation.

SCENE #1: 12 Years a Slave

In a delirious drunken stupor, Master Epps staggers into the slave quarters demanding that the slaves wake up to celebrate. He insists they come to the big house and dance, even though they've worked like animals all day and it's way late into the evening. The slaves assume the exploitive position in the middle of the floor waiting on instruction from Epps. Solomon begins to play the violin and the slaves warily dance, while the intoxicated Epps sits and watches with whip in hand. As the slaves dance, Epps' lustful eyes are glued on Patsey, on every twirl of her black body. Truth is, watching Patsey dance is the only reason for these late-night self-serving shenanigans. Mistress Epps ain't no fool; she knows exactly why her husband ordered the slaves to dance in the wee hours of the night. Finally, she can't take it anymore! She picks up a carafe and hurls it at Patsey, hitting her in the face. The music stops and there's Patsey lying on the floor with blood dripping from her face. Mistress Epps is in a jealous rage and screaming like a mad woman.

Deadly Dialogue: The Language of White Woman Violence

Mistress Epps: *Sell her!*

Epps: *C'mon on now, what's this?*

Mistress Epps: *You will sell the negress!*

Epps: *You're talkin' foolish. Sell little Pats? She pick with more vigor than any other nigger! Choose another ta go.*

Mistress Epps: *No other. Sell her!*

Epps: *I will not!*

Mistress Epps: *You will remove that black bitch from this property, er I'll take myself back to Cheneyville.*

Epps: *Back to that hog's trough where I found you? Oh, the idleness of that yarn washes over me. Do not set yourself up against Patsey, my dear. That's a wager on which you will not profit. Calm yerself. And settle for my affection, 'cause my affection you got. Or, go. 'Cause I will rid myself of yah well before I do away with her!*The legacy of White Woman Violence towards blck folks goes as far back as 1619, when the first twenty

Africans arrived in Jamestown, Virginia (according to white history). The sadistic system of chattel slavery spread like wildfire; it's estimated that six to seven million Africans were enslaved in the eighteenth century alone. African slaves, aka "Black Gold," became the property of white Americans, including white women.

White women have *always* been active participants in the captivity, degradation, and dehumanization of our black lives. The "Misses" has always been violent towards black women, and it was on the plantation she mastered her *Weapons of Whiteness*. White women have *never* been our sisters. Do not be fooled. White women are the cornerstones of the building of White Supremacy. They are stockholders with significant investments in the sociopathic system that still attacks, violates, and oppresses you and me today.

The history books don't thoroughly document and illuminate White Woman Violence as they rightfully should, instead, they place almost all of the blame for racist violence on white men. There is no doubt that white men have committed horrific crimes against black and brown humanity, and there is equally no doubt that white woman stood by, watched it happen, and did not collectively intervene to end and eliminate the horror. White women continue to be accomplices in those crimes. They have blood on their hands while denying the crimes exist. Continuing with *12 Years a Slave* as the backdrop to the legacy of White Woman Violence, the deadly dialogue illustrates the innate lack of empathy for black life and shows the brutal lethality of a fearful white woman and her violent language.

SCENE #2: 12 Years a Slave

Patsey is Master Epps' favorite slave because she can pick five hundred pounds of cotton a day and because he rapes her at will. In this scene, Patsey done ran off. Master Epps chases around the plantation looking for her like a love-crazed maniac, but she's nowhere to be found. As Patsey strolls onto the property, Master Epps screams, "You miserable wench! *Where have you been?*" Patsey first attempts to lie about her whereabouts, but then admits to going to the neighboring home of Mistress Shaw to get a small piece of soap. She is crying for her life and begging for mercy as she explains that

Mistress Epps refuses to give her soap to wash her body with. Master Epps, filled with rage and jealousy, instructs another slave to go get the whip. Master Epps doesn't believe Patsey. He thinks she's been sleeping around with another slave man.

Like the pathetic coward he is, Epps demands that Solomon beat Patsey. Mistress Epps comes outside and heartlessly perfects the white woman gaze. Like a vulture, she stands there all statuesque with callous contempt for Patsey, brooding with envy and seeking hateful satisfaction. Solomon can't bring himself to violently beat Patsey. He eventually and begrudgingly strikes Patsey with the whip, but not to the satisfaction of Mistress Epps. She isn't feeling gratified by Solomon's mercy for Patsey and her husband's failure to disprove his sick and twisted affection for Patsey.

Deadly Dialogue: The Language of White Woman Violence

Epps: *Strip her. Strike her bare 'n lash her to the post.*

Mistress Epps: *Do it! Strike the life from her.*

Epps: *Beat her.*

Mistress Epps: *He pantomimes. There ain't barely a welt on her. That's what your niggers make of yah; a fool fer the takin'. Epps becomes furious and draws a pistol on the other slaves.*

Epps: *Yah will strike her. Yah will strike her until her flesh is rent and meat and blood flow equal, or I will kill every nigger in my sight!*

Master Epps is dissatisfied with Solomon's merciful lashes, but only because his hovering, raving wife continues to berate, emasculate and provoke him. He grabs the whip from Solomon and ferociously beats Patsey until flesh is ripped from her body and she is bloody, breathless, and barely alive. Finally, Mistress Epps feels temporarily exonerated. She whisks away to the big house fulfilled with sadistic redemption. Patsey lifelessly remains tied naked to the beating post.

THIS is what White Woman Violence looked like then, and what it still looks like now. From as far back as seeing the Mister sneak out to the slave quarters in the middle of the night, to watching their husbands barbarically beat and mutilate black bodies, to chopping off Native children's hair and beating the "savage" out of them, white women have always been violent directly and indirectly. White Woman Violence no matter when it occurs, is cruel complicity, sadistic silence, fraudulent feminism, dangerous docility and deep-seated anti-black racism. White women exude a tangible coldness and palpable disgust for black women still today.

For the past year, I've been asking this question in my mind, to friends, and on social media; *Has there ever been a time in history when white women collectively, undeniably, and aggressively spoke up for and/or stood up for women of color?* I'm not talking about a few notable white women, or about a few groups of white women here and there. I'm talking about thousands and millions of white women collectively marching in the streets to say, *"No more mistreatment and oppression of women of color!"* Can you think of a time? Do you know of a time when white women collectively risked their lives to save the lives of black and brown women, a time when they sacrificed their collective time, money, resources, and energy to fight the system that oppresses women of color? Nah! There is no such time! Not even today.

Why has there never been a time when any of this happened? Because white women *know* they benefit from and are protected by White Supremacy whether they admit it or not. They *know* they have privileges and advantages that black and brown women do not. They know this deep down inside no matter how much they deny it. Collectively, white women believe they are superior to black, brown, and Native women. And why wouldn't they? Society has told them so ever since they took their first breath. White women can go anywhere and be viewed (and treated) as innocent, fragile, entitled, and superior. Even poor white women can do this.

White Woman Violence is as old as tea, as my late grandmother used to say. In other words, as long as white women have existed, *Weapons of Whiteness* has existed, too. White women don't know any other way to show up in the world unless they are on a daily Journey to Allyship; otherwise, you can expect white women in one way or another to reach down into their lethal arsenal of weapons and draw them on you at any given moment. Why do they do this? Because they can and because they've been taught how to do it well by their grandmothers, mothers, sisters, aunts, and all the other white women in their life. It's a family tradition and a violent heirloom they will pass down to their white daughters, sisters, and nieces.

These *Weapons of Whiteness* are real. They are debilitating, devastating and deadly. I'm highly confident that you have been wounded by these weapons, or that you will be at some point in your life. It's inevitable. *Weapons of Whiteness* are part of white women's history and legacy. In the next few chapters, I will explain more about these weapons and their wrath in detail. For now, let me ask you a few questions to help you better understand what I mean by White Woman Violence.

1. *Have you ever had a white woman treat you as if you were invisible?*
2. *Have you ever had a white woman ask you why you talk about racism so much?*
3. *Have you ever had a white woman cut in front of you at the checkout while shopping and then get pissed when you call her out on it?*
4. *Have you ever had a white woman touch your hair, attempt to touch your hair and or ask you ridiculous questions about your hair?*
5. *Have you ever had a white woman ask you to explain what your racial experience in life is like?*
6. *Have you ever had a white woman cry when you talk about racism?*
7. *Have you ever had a white woman speak over you or for you while you're speaking?*
8. *Have you ever had a white woman get mad at you because you won't teach her how not to be racist?*
9. *Have you ever had a white woman deny or minimize the racism you experience?*
10. *Have you ever had a white woman say, "I don't see your color; I see you"?*

How many YES responses did you have? These are common examples of the weaponry white women use to deny and minimize their racism, assault your melanin and dehumanize and trivialize your existence and racial experiences. I could have listed one hundred more *Weapons of Whiteness*, and I still wouldn't have covered them all.

Maybe you've had some great, decent, or fair relationships with white women. Maybe you've even called them friend. Maybe you've trusted white women. And maybe you haven't. When I was in my teens, twenties, and thirties, I don't recall ever having what I'd call a "real" white woman friend. I've had countless acquaintances, but no real, ride-or-die friends. And now that I'm well into my forties, I don't think it's possible for me personally. Relationships with white women require a lot of emotional labor.

All relationships require a certain amount of emotional labor, which is loosely defined as the process of managing one's feelings and expressions to fulfill a job requirement. This definition does absolutely no justice to the emotional labor needed to be in relationship with white women. In relationships, each person has a role or a job to fulfill as partner, lover, friend, and/or colleague. And part of that role is not only managing and regulating your own feelings, but, also regulating the feelings of the person you're in relationship with, which is a simplified definition of emotional intelligence. What's dramatically different in relationships with white women is the *power + privilege + prejudice* (aka, racism) dynamic.

This power dynamic makes relationships with white women problematic (although they may be possible with a lot of work). For example, if you were verbally or emotionally abused by your neighbor friend from kindergarten until you graduated from high school, how willing might you be to say yes to a friendship in college? I don't know about you, but I wouldn't be eager to start a relationship with them; if I did, I'd be non-trusting, vigilant, and quite protective of my emotional energy. This hypothetical neighbor friend has already shown me for years how she intends to treat me. Why should I believe that she's going to stop abusing me now that we're in college? There is a profound and identifiable power dynamic evidenced in this relationship.

This power dynamic creates an automatic oppressor-and-oppressed relationship. How willing would you be to put in the effort and emotional energy to "teach" your neighborhood friend how to stop abusing and oppressing you? How much energy would you give to educating this "friend" about what it means to be oppressed? Isn't it her responsibility to identify her oppression and learn how to NOT abuse and oppress you and others? Wouldn't it be laborious and exhausting for you to do this work for her? Wouldn't you be re-traumatized every time you had to educate her on her oppressive ways? Of course it would. This is what emotional labor looks like when there is a power dynamic. It is NOT your job, role or responsibility to educate or teach white women how to NOT racially oppress you.

Nine out of ten engagements or discussions with white women on how they are racist, violent, and/or oppressive always include Weapons of Whiteness being drawn. You will always be asked to exert emotional labor. You will be exhausted, and this exhaustion is abusive. I want you to allow this next statement to really sink into your consciousness. I mean let it sink in real deep. One of the truths I share with white women is this. When white women or expect women of color to teach them how to NOT to be racist, oppressive, or violent, this is what they are saying to you: **"Teach me how to NOT abuse you while I abuse you and deny that I'm abusing you."** This statement and expectation is vicious. It's downright diabolical!

[Trigger Warning] Visualize this: A man slapping a woman in the face over and over while saying, *"I really want to learn how to stop hitting you."* Hit after hit he says, *"Please teach me how to be non-violent!"* And when you try to tell him exactly what to do, he says, *"Well, it's your fault I can't learn. If you'd teach me with a nicer tone maybe I could hear you."* When white women are not actively working to uproot and eradicate their racism and working to disarm their weapons, the same thing happens. If you've ever tried to have a conversation about racism with a white woman who is NOT doing her work, then you know exactly what I mean. You know how emotionally abusive, depleting, and exhausting it is. Making such an attempt is a waste of your emotional energy. This is what emotional labor looks like in real life.

White Woman Violence is as natural and plentiful as the air they breathe. Just like *The Rose* I described at the beginning of the book, white women will *always* have thorns. Can you have genuine, trusting relationships with them? Well, I don't know if it's possible, but it's sure not necessary. Even if you choose to not have personal and intimate relationships with white women, you will have to learn how to deal with all the violent and oppressive variations of their Beckyness! Becky ain't going anywhere! She's here to stay. And in order for you to stay mentally well, you have to learn how to resist and thrive in the face of Beckyism. If Becky won't lay down her weapons you must learn how to arm yourself with the mental and emotional tools so you can not only survive, but thrive and experience deep, rich, abundant joy! You need to master *The Becky Code!*

Cracking the BECKY Code Clues

Becky's Weapons of Whiteness are deeply engrained. Don't expect her to change overnight and be cautious all of the time.

Always trust your gut. If something doesn't feel right when you engage with Becky listen to your instincts. Remember where there's smoke there is fire.

Don't waste your magic by providing Becky with emotional labor. You don't owe her anything!

Don't Waste Your Magic: What have you learned about Becky?

_____

_____

_____

_____

_____

_____

_____

" Nobody is **as powerful as we** make them out to **be. "**

-Alice Walker

CHAPTER TWO

Miss Anne,
Becky, and Rachel

"If you are silent about your pain, they'll kill you and say you enjoyed it."
– Zora Neal Hurston

Becky will kill you softly with her words, pretend she doesn't know what's happening, and blame you for your slow emotional death. Talking about racism and oppression with white women will go one of two ways: either they will agitate you with their racial ignorance, or they will refresh you with words of understanding and nourishment. There really is no gray area in these conversations. White women have no idea what it's like to walk in your shoes. They've been sheltered from the harsh realities of your struggles, even if they've often been the instigators and perpetrators of your pain. Occasionally, you may encounter a white woman who is on what I call the *Journey to Allyship,* and she'll "get it" as much as a white woman can. In this instance, she may not start out agitating, but if you engage long enough, Becky will eventually tick you off and draw her weapons.

There's more than one definition of Becky, and dealing with Becky and all of her problematic personas and White Woman Violence is maddening and exhausting. The first step in cracking *The Becky Code* is to know who Becky really is so you can disarm her effectively with the least amount of emotional labor. Becky has existed since the beginning of time; we just didn't have a name for her. Because calling her "Becky" is fairly new (within the last twenty or thirty years), you may know her by a different name: *Miss Anne!* I've been hearing about Miss Anne since I was a young girl, but I didn't really know who or what that was. My grandmother and mother used to call certain white women "Miss Anne," and it clearly wasn't from a place of affection.

Miss Anne

Miss Anne. She is painfully unforgettable! You will know for sure when you encounter her: arrogant, uppity, condescending, and downright *stank* and imperious in her attitude. I know you've encountered and engaged with some Miss Annes in your life, right? We all have, and yes, they get on our damn nerves! Often prim and proper, snooty and slick with her racist undertones, Miss Anne doesn't have a problem letting you know she has a problem with YOU, black or brown woman. When I think of the epitome of Miss Anne, the character Miss Millie from *The Color Purple* comes to vividly to mind.

If you've seen the movie *The Color Purple,* you know the scene I'm talking about. Miss Millie, a white woman and the mayor's wife, imposes herself all up in Sofia's (Oprah Winfrey's character's) face while Sofia is minding her own business. Miss Millie intrudes on Sofia's day off by touching Sofia's children without permission, and then commenting on how "clean" they are (as if she expected them to be dirty). Miss Millie then has the damn audacity to ask Sofia if she wants to work for her and be her maid! Sofia in a matter-of-fact tone of voice, boldly says, *"Hell nah!"* Ole Miss Millie, shocked and wrongfully offended, says, "What did you say?" Sofia says, "*I said, hell nah!*" The scene ends with the white mayor hitting Sofia over the head with his gun after a mob of angry white people call her derogatory names and violently beat her. Sofia ends up in jail, and upon release (after about eight years!) with a fractured skull and broken ribs, ends up being Miss Millie's maid anyway.

Miss Millie may be a fictitious character in a movie, but her vicious persona is still alive and thriving in the minds and hearts of many white women today. There's a little bit of Miss Millie in all white women that comes from a deep place of White Superiority and White Entitlement. For centuries, white women have been allowed and encouraged to believe and act as if they are better than women of color. Have you encountered this type of Antagonist before? Let me illustrate further just how selfish and violent the Miss Millies of the world can be. In my book *Antagonists, Advocates and Allies: The Wake Up Call Guide for White Women Who Want to Become Allies with Black Women,* I define the white woman Antagonist as follows:

"The Antagonist is a woman who actively opposes or is hostile to someone or something; she's argumentative, defensive, and aggressive, blames others, excludes, and just seems to make everything difficult, challenging and drama-filled."

Antagonists don't believe that White Privilege is real, and if it is, they certainly don't believe they benefit from it. A classic false belief of the Antagonist is that they are colorblind; they proudly declare that we're all human beings who are created equal. Their favorite mode of operation when engaging in race-related topics is to get defensive, with denial, justification, minimization, and rationalization as their go-to Weapons of Whiteness. (I introduced these dangerous weapons in Chapter 1; I'll provide more details and explain how you can identify and disarm them in later chapters.)

Antagonistic white women will minimize the lived racial experiences of women of color by asserting they understand your plight because they experience other forms of oppression, such as sexism or classism. And if you call them out on their racism, they will deny it and scream, "Reverse racism." Antagonists are fragile, lack the emotional stamina to engage in race talks, and often become hurt, angry, and aggressive when confronted about their racism. You'll know you're dealing with an *Antagonist* when you hear phrases from the White Woman Script such as, "Why are you making this about race, *you're* pulling the race card, I'm a good person and I'm not racist," and/or "Well, that kind of stuff happens to me, too; are you *sure* it was racially motivated?"

Do you know someone like that? She would be the perfect poster child for the *Mean Girl* campaign! Antagonists are good for using the term *reverse racism*. Antagonists quickly dismiss the truth and reality of women of color by making statements like the ones above. Here are some more; see if you recognize them: *"Don't you think you focus too much on race, why does this have to be a race issue, I don't see race or color, I just see people,"* and/or, *"It sounds like you (a person of color) have some personal issues with white people."* (And there are more where those come from; I've included other statements from the White Woman Script in upcoming chapters.) When you call an Antagonist out on their racism and violent behavior, they will behave just like Miss Millie (Miss Anne!) in *The Color Purple:* they will become startled by your audacity, transform into the victim, and drown you with manipulative White Tears.

Miss Anne *is* Becky, often an older version of Becky, perhaps Becky's aunt, mother, grandmother, or older friends. Because Miss Anne usually has no filter, she also has zero qualms about letting you know where she ignorantly stands. Miss Anne is the Becky that stares you up and down for no reason with the White Woman Gaze. Miss Anne is the Becky that turns her nose up at you because she thinks you're beneath her. Miss Anne is easy to spot with her bold, willful ignorance and racism. Although initially jarring, I'd almost rather deal with a Miss Anne, because her problematic behavior is in plain sight. Still, Miss Anne and all of her shameless shenanigans are a serious, direct threat to your emotional safety and mental wellness. There is an effective way to deal with Miss Anne. I will share how to unlearn certain behaviors in Chapter 8 in order to confidently deal with Miss Anne.

Becky

Now let's talk about *the* Becky of *all* Beckys. Girl! What's wrong with Becky? You know who Becky is. Becky is your typical, often mediocre, on the low, "I'm not racist," racist white woman who is clueless to the propensity of her White Woman Privilege and "modern day" (subtle racism) racism. Becky would proudly describe herself as liberal, progressive, socially conscious, and an all-around "good" white woman who gets it (racism). She'll make sure you know that her best friend (now in college or high school) is black or brown, or perhaps she's married to a person of color, or her children or nieces and nephews are biracial or multiracial. In other words, she will tell you all of the reasons she is NOT racist. Reasons I'm sure you've heard a million times before, right? Predictable and exhausting!

Becky believes she is a well-intentioned white woman who thinks she knows more about racism and oppression than you do. She's read some books, watched a few documentaries, and perhaps has participated in some kind of diversity training. Oblivious to what racism really is, Becky distances herself from "those bad racists" out there and insists she one of the *good ones*, while simultaneously launching every weapon in her arsenal at will (White Superiority, White Authority, White Entitlement, White Denial, and

White Innocence, to name a few). Some Beckys proudly wear the badge of "we're all human." They'll trivialize your pain with offensive offerings of love and light while demanding you stay positive and talk nice about your oppression.

Speaking of talking nice, Becky will tone police the hell out of you! She will assume you are addressing her when you make general comments about racism. She will interrupt your conversations, talk over you, and speak for you. She will interrogate you with a thousand questions and answer them for you. She will tell you to stop complaining, to look on the bright side, and will often play devil's advocate, which is a way to say racist sh!t on the down low. She will declare that you're attacking her when you call out her racism. She will say your words (or you) are blaming and shaming her. She will demand you watch your tone when speaking to her, and she will remind you that you could better articulate your point if you'd only speak nicely. And her favorite tone policing tactic is the expectation that you'll pull her to the side to call out her racism privately.

Becky is annoying, apathetic, and exhausting. She is problematic in so many dangerous ways. One of the most detrimental characteristics of Becky is that she is complicit in your oppression by what I call *willful ignorance* and *silent knowing*. Sometimes when I engage with white women who have not started their Journey to Allyship, I'm curious about what reality they actually live in. Many white women claim they don't understand the struggles of black, brown, Native, and Indigenous women. Although there may be some truth there, I believe deep down inside they DO know what is happening to us. There are two questions you can ask a white woman to discover her truth: 1) If you could live the rest of your life as a black woman, would you? and 2) Would you be willing to be treated the way black people are treated by society?

I asked these two questions as informal research to a group of about forty white women in an online course I offer. They agreed to respond honestly to the questions to help illustrate my point that they do know what is happening to black, brown, Native, and Indigenous women. The questions were posed exactly as written above. Many of the responses were similar in nature; here is a compilation of the answers I received:

- No. I wouldn't live the rest of my life as a black woman because of the additional challenges it would bring navigating in a racist society. No. I wouldn't be willing to be treated the way black people are treated in this country.
- No. I am not prepared to live the rest of my life as a black woman. I do not have the strength to be treated the way black people are treated. I would love to experience the love of the black community, but I wouldn't want to be black. I can feel the racism in my answer deep in my heart.
- No. I am not ready. I am still too racist. It would not be genuine. It would be blackface at best and fetishizing at worst. I refuse to be like Rachel Dolezal.
- No. I do not have the fortitude to live each moment in this racist society. I would crumble.
- No. I wouldn't want to live the rest of my life as a black woman. It would be a lie. It would be fetishisization. No. I couldn't tolerate being treated like black people are in this country. It's violence.

I was not shocked by these answers. They confirmed two of my conclusions about the collective white woman. First, they KNOW what is happening to black, brown, Native, and Indigenous women and are not doing anything, or enough, about it. This is the *silent knowing* and *willful ignorance* I mentioned earlier. Second, if they chose to be black women for the duration of their lives, it would be only for the perceived positive attributes of our character and life experiences. Collectively, white women don't give a damn about us, and that's why there has NEVER been a time in history when they have put their privilege, money, time, resources, and lives on the line to stop the racist violence against us.

Unless you choose to become a separatist (and I know a few women who are), you'll have to deal with Becky's Beckyism in all of its violent Beckery. There's a Becky for every occasion, situation, and encounter you have with white women. It doesn't matter how far along they are in their anti-racist journey. At some point, white women will minimize you, disappoint you, and use their Weapons of Whiteness against you. I could describe all the Beckys

I've encountered, and I still wouldn't capture the breadth of Beckyism you'll deal with in your lifetime. What I know for sure is that you will encounter at least one, if not all, of these Beckys:

"Nah, Not Today Becky!"

Super Becky: A savior-complex Becky who is notorious for jumping into conversations about racism to Save-A-Black or Brown woman without their consent.

Begging Becky: A performative Becky who is always sniffing around, panting for pats on the back, and begging for Ally Cookies (accolades and praise).

Wanna-Be-Black Becky: A Becky who loves to date black men/women, fetishizes black women, and appropriates AAVE to appear "woke."

Talk-Too-Damn-Much Becky: A talkative, centering Becky who adds no value, validity, or validation in race talks.

Know-It-All Becky: A condescending, apathetic Becky who intellectualizes racism by using a cognitive approach to understanding and discussing racism.

Love-and-Light Becky: An oblivious Becky who selfishly uses a sprinkling of love, light, and woo-woo talk to avoid facing her racism and to minimize your oppression.

Whining-Ass Becky: The most fragile Becky of all. She's perpetually hurt about anything and everything related to racism. She's a master at crying a river of White Tears.

Ole-Thieving-Ass Becky: A Becky who rapes and robs the culture of black and brown people to create an identity so she can feel alive inside.

Get-On-Your-Nerves Becky: A Becky who just gets on your nerves. She's a combination of Talk-Too-Damn-Much Becky and Know-It-All Becky, and she will exhaust the hell out of you.

Coworker Becky: A Becky who smiles in your face and tries to sabotage your success at work.

BWAM Becky (But What About Me?): A Becky whose favorite Weapon of Whiteness is Centering. She becomes fragile and defensive when she's not getting all of the attention.

At any given moment, you can expect Becky to withdraw, cry, defend, project, dismiss, agitate, ignore, attack, deny, and/or retaliate. Becky will be Becky. I do believe that white women can be less oppressive, less violent, and less harmful; however, Beckyism is a serious addiction for white women. You may think Beckyism can't get any worse than the behaviors mentioned above, but oh yes, it can. Let me introduce you to the Becky of all Beckys: Rachel.

Rachel

Rachel. Rachel. Rachel! My mind is still blown by the one and only Rachel Dolezal. For many years Rachel, a white woman, who now identifies as trans-black, lived as a black woman in Spokane, Washington. With some kinky hair, a tan, and the theft of African-American Vernacular English (AAVE, pronounced *ah-vay*), Rachel was able to deceive the black community into believing she was a black woman. So much so that she became the head of her local NAACP chapter, used her violent boldness to slither her way into the African American Studies department at Eastern Washington University. This thieving Becky had the damn nerve to teach a class called, "The Black Woman's Struggle." What the hell! Rachel isn't the first white woman to successfully pass as black and she certainly won't be the last.

What's most offensive about Rachel is that she claims to be trans-racial. What the hell is that? It's violence, that's what. She believes and feels as if she is black on the inside and therefore has the right to pretend to BE black. This is the ultimate act of White Privilege violence. Rachel is oblivious to what it really means to be a black woman. It is certainly way more than rocking an afro and sporting a horrible tan. She's clueless to what living in black skin means. How dare she try on "blackness" and perpetrate a fraud just because she feels like it. What a violent slap in the face to black women!

The question is, why? Why did Rachel do this? What compelled Rachel to commit years of blackface and the fetishization of black women? When you research photographs of Rachel's childhood and young adult years, you'll clearly see a white woman with white parents. Rachel will, however, vehemently deny her whiteness and insist that although she is the daughter of two white parents she is black on the inside. She feels like a black woman. What the what? What does that even feel like, and as a white woman, how would she know? Again, why would Rachel do this? The simple answer is, because she *can*, because white supremacy and White Privilege allow her to do so. Rachel is the worst kind of Becky, the most violent Becky of all.

Rachel takes Wanna-Be-Black Becky to the ultimate offense. She assumed the perceived lifestyle of black women, raped the culture, and called it her own. But no matter how hard Rachel tries, she will *never* be a black woman. Period. Since being exposed as a lying impersonator, Rachel has had the audacity to change her name to Nkechi Amare Diallo, an African name that means *bold gift from God*. In my opinion, *bold* is a gross understatement. Rachel Dolezal may think she looks like a black woman, and maybe she can regurgitate AAVE, yet she is void of the essential characteristic, the *soul* of a black woman. No external adornments and language appropriation will *ever* make Rachel BECKY Dolezal a black woman.

Finally, in 2015, Rachel was exposed, condemned by many, and ostracized almost into obscurity. An interviewer one day asked her if she was African American? He showed her a picture of her white father and asked whether that was indeed her father. She nervously said yes, began to panic, and eventually refused to answer any more questions. Rachel denied allegations of being an ethnic fraud and the Rachel Dolezal scandal ensued. She experienced a social steamrolling, and yet the most violent Becky of them all felt no shame or guilt, and refused to take full responsibility for her actions. In fact, she dug her heels in deeper.

Rachel was not able to secure work, the community no longer trusted her, and many of her close friends, colleagues, and family abandoned her for her transgressions. At one point she was broke, homeless, and hopeless. In other words, she was facing struggles similar to the ones black women face every day. You'd think that in that moment of despair, Rachel might have caught a sliver of a glimpse into the real challenges black women experience daily. But nah, not Rachel BECKY Dolezal! This Becky chose to continue to perpetrate fraudulent violence by flouncing around on talk shows, doing interviews about her trans-racial identity, and then writing a book to tell her story of lies. Yes, I know there are black folks who don't see Rachel's con as racial violence, and that's okay. But I do. Rachel committed the vilest Beckery of all: she was born into her White Privilege, which allowed her to choose to pretend to be black.

I've seen Beckery of this kind too many times to count. I've never personally met a white woman who took her violence as far as Rachel, but I've sure encountered many who were fetishizing blackness to the point of exclusively dating black men, rocking "black" hairstyles, speaking better AAVE than I do, exclusively hanging out with my black sisters like they are *their* Sistahs, hanging out at all the black people events, mimicking what they perceive to be black girl mannerisms, dropping the N-bomb left and right, and doing everything in between to appropriate black culture and commit a mockery of black women. This is the Becky that works my nerves the most. I have zero tolerance for this violence, and zero interest in ever befriending *this* kind of Becky.

What the Beck! *Miss Anne, Becky,* and *Rachel* have very real thoughts, beliefs, actions, and personas that wreak hell and havoc in the lives of black, brown, Native, and Indigenous women's lives. We may joke about all the variations of Beckery we endure, yet this Beckyism is a detriment to our spiritual, emotional, psychological, and literal selves. Beckery is dismissive, accusatory, manipulative, diabolical, damaging, and yes, extremely violent.

Just like *The Rose* and her thorns, I don't know if it's possible to engage with white women without experiencing some form of Beckery. I work from home, so I'm not exposed to many white women on a daily basis. However, part of my social and racial justice work is specifically geared toward white women. I host in-person workshops and online courses just for white women. Why? First, as much as white women anger and frustrate me, I do not *hate* them.

I grew up in a small town in Iowa, so I'm very familiar with Becky and her weapons. I've been dealing with the Beckery all my life. Second, I believe in going straight to the source to solve problems. For centuries, white women have been allowed to fly under the radar of white supremacy. They sit back and let white men take the majority of blame for racism and violence against black, brown, Native, and Indigenous people.

I hold white women accountable for their racist statements and behaviors. If they don't bother me, I don't bother them. But as Congresswoman Maxine Waters says, *"If you come for me, I'm coming for you."* And in my workshops and courses, I tell the participants, "You have been privileged for far too long and have had **your** say when it comes to gender and race. TODAY is the day that you sit down and listen without interrupting, projecting, minimizing, denying, blaming, justifying, or becoming offended and defensive. YOUR White Fragility pass has been revoked. It has expired and shall NOT be renewed." When my class is in session, the expectation is for white women to sit down, be quiet, and listen.

White women have had centuries of opportunities to express how they feel, to say what they want, and to impose their privileged views, values, rules, guidelines, and experiences onto women of color. But in my work with them, I am the teacher. I call them out on their racism unapologetically, which most often causes them to be pissed, offended, appalled, or hurt by the unfiltered truth about their Weapons of Whiteness. I make it clear that I don't need or want their sympathy or apology, I won't be considering any of the other "Isms" they face, and none of them get any passes.

All white women have and lethally use Weapons of Whiteness. I know you've felt their wrath. I know you're frustrated, tired, and angry. Keep calling out this violence. Keep speaking up and reclaiming your power, because as

Zora Neale Hurston says, "If you are silent about your pain, *they'll kill you and say you enjoyed it.*" Keep reading. There is healing balm in this book for your Racial Battle Fatigue.

Cracking the BECKY Code Clues

Remember, it doesn't matter what kind of Becky you encounter; they are all addicted to Beckyism and will use Weapons of Whiteness against you.

Never be silent about your pain and the violence that Becky inflicts on you. Speak up and call out her violence.

When dealing with Becky, it's important for you to learn how her whiteness triggers you. Identify the forms of Beckyism that irritate you and attack your emotional well-being the most so that you know how to respond and protect yourself.

Don't Waste Your Magic: How will you address Becky's violence?

_____

_____

_____

_____

_____

_____

_____

"It's not the **load** that **breaks you** down, it's the **way** you carry it.**"**
-Lena Horne

CHAPTER THREE

The toxic **Truth** **about** White Women

"Caring for **myself** is not self-indulgence, it is self-preservation, and that is an act of political warfare." – Audre Lorde

---

Racial Battle Fatigue, a term coined by William A. Smith, Department Chair of the Department of Education, Culture & Society at the University of Utah, is a REAL psychophysiological condition. Maybe you've experienced Racial Battle Fatigue, but didn't have words to describe the cumulative psychosocial, racial invalidations, insults, assaults, and microaggressions (also known as *racial invalidations*) you've experienced all your life. In other words, you didn't have the language for what you've felt in those moments when white people have dismissed you and your pain, followed you in the store, ignored your presence, asked racially inappropriate questions, and/or stereotyped and discriminated against you.

Racial Battle Fatigue is the result of dealing with a barrage of psychological transactions drenched in white supremacy, racism, oppression, White Fragility, and Beckyism. The nature of these transactions or engagements with white people, white women in particular, is interpersonal violence. The toxic truth about white women is that they have been inflicting interpersonal violence, also known as *White Woman Violence*, on women of color since forever through the use of *Weapons of Whiteness*. These weapons are the riot gear that white women carry around and discharge on the daily. This isn't a new thing; the feminist movement is rooted in White Woman Violence and Beckyism.

Do you know how racist the heralds Susan B. Anthony and Elizabeth Cady Stanton were? And they weren't the only racist feminists. While doing some research for my book *White Spaces Missing Faces: Why Women of Color Don't Trust White Women*, I discovered just how racist the white mothers of the feminist movement really were. Here's a passage I share in that book about the vile white supremacy openly displayed by leaders of the women's movement.

In my quest for answers, I've come to strongly believe that feminism is White Feminism. It was never designed to include, uplift, fight for, and empower all women. Its historical roots are anchored in racism and hatred of black women and men, and even today, feminism as we know it is exclusive and collectively unsupportive of anyone who lives in the margins of straight, cis-gender, heterosexual white women. Two of the women's movements founders, Susan B. Anthony and Elizabeth Cady Stanton, were the epitome of the White Antagonistic woman. In fact, Susan B. Anthony states the following quote during her time advocating for women to get the right to vote "*I will cut off this right arm of mine before I will ask for the ballot for the Negro and not for the woman.*"

Susan B. Anthony wasn't alone in her racism and disdain for black people. Several of the early women's right activists were not interested in including all women in their quest for equality. Some of them were downright racist and nasty in their response to the idea of equal treatment for not only black and brown women, but also black men in particular. Here's how many of them felt in their own words:

- "*You have put the ballot in the hands of your black men, thus making them political superiors of white women. Never before in the history of the world have men made former slaves the political masters of their former mistresses!*" -- Anna Howard Shaw

- "*The enfranchisement of women would insure immediate and durable white supremacy, honestly attained, for upon unquestioned authority it is stated that in every southern State but one there are more educated women than all the illiterate voters, white and black, native and foreign, combined. As you probably know, of all the women in the South who can read and write, ten out of every eleven are white. When it comes to the proportion of property between the races, that of the white outweighs that of the black immeasurably.*" -- Belle Kearney

- "*What will we and our daughters suffer if these degraded black men are allowed to have the rights that would make them even worse than our Saxon fathers?*" -- Elizabeth Cady Stanton

- *"The white men, reinforced by the educated white women, could 'snow under' the Negro vote in every State, and the white race would maintain its supremacy without corrupting or intimidating the Negroes."* --Laura Clay

- *"Alien illiterates rule our cities today; the saloon is their palace, and the toddy stick their scepter. The colored race multiplies like the locusts of Egypt."* -- Frances Willard

- *"White supremacy will be strengthened, not weakened, by women's suffrage."* -- Carrie Chapman Catt

- *"I do not want to see a negro man walk to the polls and vote on who should handle my tax money, while I myself cannot vote at all...When there is not enough religion in the pulpit to organize a crusade against sin; nor justice in the court house to promptly punish crime; nor manhood enough in the nation to put a sheltering arm about innocence and virtue—-if it needs lynching to protect woman's dearest possession from the ravening human beasts—-then I say lynch, a thousand times a week if necessary."* -- Rebecca Ann Latimer Felton

These are the toxic roots of feminism. Unfortunately, feminism as we know it today is not much different than it was a century ago. *The Women's March on Washington* that took place in January, 2017 proved once again that white women *must* be in the front, at the center, and leading the way with *their* agendas; which is not an agenda for *all* women.

When white women are NOT the center of attention, and when they are called out on their exclusionary and selfish behaviors, they WILL draw their weapons. White women like Anthony, Cady Stanton, and Clay, mentioned above, were the Beckys of yesterday. Times have changed, those women have passed on, but Beckyism is alive and kicking in the feminist movement and women's empowerment circles. As you can see, Beckyism shows up in a lot of different behaviors even when white women are on the Journey to Allyship.

In Chapter 2, I described the different Becky personas. Now I'll go a little deeper and point out some distinctions of Beckyism. This will help you know exactly who and what you're dealing with when you experience interpersonal violence while engaging with white women. In *White Spaces Missing Faces,* I define the characteristics and behaviors of Antagonists, Advocates, Allies, and Accomplices to illustrate how white women show up in the lives of women of color. Here's an excerpt:

Antagonists, Advocates and Allies

An **Antagonist** is a white woman who claims to not see color; she believes she is not racist and denies having white privilege. She usually justifies her disbelief by sharing examples of her own struggles and oppression. She believes we are one race, the human race and doesn't understand why there is so much talk about racism. Her definition of racism is explicit, and she fails to or refuses to admit to her own implicit racial biases and racism. Her perception of racism is blatant examples and overt hateful behaviors. She has difficulty or refuses to acknowledge the nuances of racism and the insidious ways in which racism can be perpetrated.

An Antagonist is a woman of color's worst living nightmare. She is offensive and insensitive to a woman of color's lived racial experiences. She has great difficulty talking about race, racism and white privilege without becoming angry, defensive, or emotional. Antagonists are consistently notorious for minimizing racism, committing racial microaggressions and expecting to be educated by black and brown women and becomes passive-aggressive and sometimes openly aggressive, when women of color refuse her demands. Antagonists cry the most white tears. They are very emotionally fragile during discussions about race and racism, they fail to take responsibility for their actions and will fight relentlessly to prove they are not racist.

And finally, Antagonists ultimately perpetuate racism by demonstrating the aforementioned behaviors along with frequently proclaiming reverse-racism when women of color confront their oppressive behavior. Antagonists don't know how to and or refuse to validate a person of color's experiences by centering themselves in the conversation or during a personal engagement when racism is the topic at hand. They are master manipulators and frequently derail the conversation by shifting the focus onto their feelings and needs.

Antagonists are always operating from a manipulative and abusive bag of tricks that include denial, minimization, justification, rationalization, blame shifting and derailment. Antagonists are just that. They antagonize women of color at every turn, yet truly believe they are "good people" who do no harm.

Advocates are white women who know that racism exists, believe it's wrong and are conscious enough to not explicitly act out their implicit biases. They may also believe in the colorblind approach when engaging with others yet have a moderate desire to talk about race and racism. They are not necessarily against women of color, yet their behaviors don't outright show they are for women of color neither. Advocates are primarily on the fence about racial justice work. They see racism and injustice and want to speak up, but they are afraid to make mistakes and don't know how to go about it.

Fear is their greatest motivator and deterrent. They are afraid to confront other white people about their racism for fear they may lose a friend, a family member or upset a co-worker. Advocates do not want to make waves or ruffle feathers yet inside they want to. Advocates also know they have implicit biases and often lurk in the shadows attempting to soak up knowledge and wisdom about racism and how to overcome it. They often ask people of color to teach them how, yet don't understand that asking is a racist act in and of itself. When people of color refuse or fail to teach them they often resort back to sitting on the fence. They feel a sense of "I'm dammed if I do, and I'm dammed if I don't."

Beyond fear, Advocates are often driven or paralyzed by shame and guilt. They often feel shame about how racism has destroyed lives and dehumanized people, and, because they have white skin, they experience and hold on to guilt. Neither of these responses are helpful, and they often help keep Advocates on the fence about taking action. And finally, Advocates want to be allies, but their fear of being confronted about racism is more powerful than their desire to get uncomfortable in order to become an Ally. Advocates are dangerous; they're unpredictable and unreliable for people of color. They are neutral, and, when one chooses to be neutral, they have sided with the oppressor. In order for women of color to thrive in white spaces, they need Allies and Accomplices.

Allies are white women who have accepted and owned their racism and are doing the personal inner work to continuously uproot racist behaviors and implicit biases. They are not afraid to call racism out and or call out people who behave in racist ways. They recognize and accept they have unearned white privilege and are innately prone to white fragility. They have chosen to use their power and privilege to stand up to social and racial injustices. They've done (and are doing continuously) extensive inner work to uproot and eliminate the white fragility, which they know is a form of violence against people of color.

Allies are not paralyzed by fear, shame or guilt, and they take daily action to continue to dismantle their own internalized dominance and perceived superiority. They refuse to be silent and are comfortable breaking up and or disrupting white spaces that exclude, marginalize and oppress people of color. They not only challenge racism on a personal level, they intentionally and consistently challenge and defy white supremacy and institutional and structural systemic racism at every level. This means they are questioning and challenging leaders, lawmakers, people in positions of power, laws, rules (formal and informal), policies, procedures, beliefs, practices and protocols that favor white people and oppress people of color.

One of the most important behaviors for Allies to consistently demonstrate is listening more than they speak, especially when engaging with women of color. Although racism was created by white people for white people and white people benefit from it, people of color know *more* about racism than white people, and Allies know and agree with this truth. Allies know they should never attempt to "educate" people of color about racism and that to do so is racist. People of color on a daily basis fight against racism and racist people which results in Racial

Battle Fatigue.

Racial Battle Fatigue manifests due to people of color experiencing daily microaggressions and other forms of explicit racial assaults. They become physically tired, irritable, emotionally exhausted from explaining, teaching and defending themselves and can experience anxiety and even mild to severe forms of depression. In other words, black and brown people get (and are) tired of dealing with racism, working to avoid racism, talking about racism, explaining racism, and experiencing racism to only be told, *"you're making it up, you're pulling the race card, you're being too sensitive, I didn't mean to offend you, how will I learn if you won't teach me"* and a forever oppressive list of unacceptable and abusive responses to racism.

Strong and effective allies know people of color experience *Racial Battle Fatigue,* and part of their role is to step in and relieve some of the fatigue by specifically challenging and working with Antagonists and Advocates. Antagonists are highly abusive to people of color, and, if Advocates aren't willing to jump off the fence, they too can create emotional exhaustion for people of color. Allies know their real work is to seek out, reach and teach white people about their racism and work to get them to uproot their racism with the ultimate goal of creating more allies. Allies, just like in times of war, are always preparing to align themselves with people of color when they are on the battle grounds of racism.

Allies don't stop fighting until the battle is won. Allies are always ready and available to support people of color and Accomplices don't wait for the call from women of color. They are actively disrupting racism in every space and place and systemically. Accomplices not only take on the role and responsibilities of an Ally, they are working in cahoots with black and brown people to intentionally, systematically and relentlessly dismantle white supremacy and racism. Accomplices are co-conspirators against racial injustice.

As with all human beings, Allies and Accomplices are not infallible; they are still capable of discharging Weapons of Whiteness and acting out violent Beckery. As I've said before, it doesn't matter how far along in the journey white women are; you are still subject to their Beckyism. Recently I experienced the Beckery of an "Ally friend" with strong undertones of Miss Anne that violently bubbled to the surface. This white woman, whom I'll call Maureen, had read my books *Antagonists, Advocates and Allies and White Spaces Missing Faces*, participated in two of my anti-racism workshops, was a participant in one of my online programs, and had been to my home on a handful of occasions. We were in the beginning stages of trying to build a friendship beyond anti-racism work.

For a little over two years we seemed to be making good progress. Maureen was doing HER work to learn how to lay down her weapons, showing up online to challenge racism, attending local anti-racism events, standing up for racial justice in real life, and being a model for what Allyship can look like when white women choose to lay down their weapons. Over the year, we had a few minor disagreements, some hard yet truthful conversations, and even managed to just enjoy each other's company and laugh a little. On a positive note, I encountered way less Beckery from Maureen than from other white women. I could be in her physical presence without experiencing weapon after weapon. My social media exchanges with her were supportive and nourishing. And then something expected, but also unexpected, happened.

Something was brewing inside Maureen. I wasn't exactly sure what it was, but I could sense it. She seemed to be distancing herself from me online, and became curt and interrogative with her responses. Our engagements became less frequent. For the most part I ignored it, but then she posted in one of my online forums and seemed to be bitter about something. I suspected it had to do with me. Whatever was brewing inside of Maureen finally surfaced, and just like that she was in full riot gear, with Weapons of Whiteness locked and loaded. Finally, it went down online. We engaged in a fiery exchange in one of my social media groups.

Essentially, Maureen was upset with me for a reason still unknown to me today. And she drew the weapons of White Superiority, White Entitlement, White Fragility, White Centering, and White Interrogation. Throughout this social media exchange, Maureen was locked into being right, proving her point, and refusing to lay down her weapons. It was clear to me that this was a personal vendetta, but I had no clue why it suddenly appeared. At some point in the conversation, Maureen questioned my leadership integrity. She also attempted to drag another white woman in the group down with her, a woman who had absolutely nothing to do with the conversation Maureen and I were having. For the first time in two years, I SAW Maureen in rare form. I saw Becky emerge with automatic weapons blazing with no interest in stopping until her clip was empty.

This was a rubber-meets-the-road point. I knew unequivocally it was the end of our relationship. All of the trust Maureen had earned over the years instantly vanished. I informed her that we had reached a point of no return, that she had crossed lines I was unwilling to reconcile, removed her from the group, and severed my relationship with her. Maureen reminded me she was a Rose with thorns that cut and draw blood. I don't know if black, brown, Native, and Indigenous women can truly have deep, personal, and intimate relationships with white women. I've never been successful at it, and Maureen reminded me that I should never forget that attempting to befriend Becky is like trying to teach a snake to not slither. Slithering is in the snake's DNA. It's what they do. It's who they are.

I do know this. I will always choose my mental wellness, emotional well-being, peace, justice, and liberation over a white woman *every single time*. Black, brown, Native, and Indigenous women do NOT have to tolerate Becky and her Beckery, ever! Haven't we been tolerating this toxic violence long enough, at the expense of our own well-being? Congresswoman Maxine Waters reminds us to RECLAIM OUR TIME, and that I will do by any means necessary. And you should, too. You are not a social experiment. You are not a toy to be played with. You are not an emotional punching bag. You are NOT a guinea pig for white people's personal research. You are a human being who deserves to be treated with respect, kindness, empathy, and compassion.

It's ironic that white women can clearly see and articulate their anger, pain, and frustration with patriarchy, sexism, and misogyny and how these "isms" silence, violate, and oppress them, but can't (or refuse to) see that toxic white feminism is equally silencing, violating, and oppressive. The very thing they despise is the very thing they are. Let me just give it to you straight: white women may loathe white male dominance, but they are protected under the impermeable cloak of white supremacy. Frankly, it's not all that ironic. I believe that white women KNOW they are collectively safeguarded by the very white male patriarchy they want to smash!

This leads me back to my initial conclusion that white women know damn well what they are doing while hiding behind the veils of feminism and White Innocence. Becky, Beckery, and Beckyism are toxic! There's simply no better word than *toxic* to articulate the depth and breadth of White Woman Violence. White women who are NOT owning and dismantling their racism and working to lay down their weapons are a detriment to our mental and emotional well-being:

- The denial of their racism is deadly.
- Their "we're all just humans and let's just love each other" mentality is harmful.
- Their refusal to identify their weapons of mass destruction is lethal.
- Every time they minimize your existence or fetishize your power, they dehumanize the essence of who you are.
- Every time white women make a racially insensitive and insulting statement, they steal a piece of your joy.
- Every time they ask you a race-related question that you've already answered a thousand times, they exhaust you and chip away at your emotional resiliency. This is undisputed toxic behavior.

Befriending Becky is not a decision to make on a whim. No matter how down, evolved, and so-called "woke" Becky is, you will be frustrated, pissed off, exhausted, and overwhelmed with her toxic Beckery. She will make you sick with Racial Battle Fatigue. Experiencing Racial Battle Fatigue will deplete you and it will cause you to more easily sink into the Sunken Place. The Sunken Place is a horrible psychological and mental state and all Beckys have the capacity to make you sink! I'll elaborate on the Sunken Place more in Chapter 7 and share how to emerge from this place of horror.

Now you might be saying, "Not ALL white women, Catrice!" And I AM saying, "Yes, my Sister, ALL white women will exhibit varying degrees of Beckyism." I've been hard-pressed to find just one white woman who is NOT Becky after four-plus decades in this black skin of mine. Becky is The Rose and The Rose is Becky. She was born with thorns. It's up to whether you choose to pick up The Rose and hold it or not. Remember that white women are toxic and always have weapons. The weapons may be invisible, but they are deadly. Be particular about who you engage with. Don't waste your magic!

Cracking the BECKY Code Clues

Listen to your body. If you feel frustrated, angry, and emotionally tired when dealing with a Becky, she's an Antagonist and detrimental to your health.

Centering is one of the top three weapons of choice for Becky. If she makes everything about her, she is not concerned with what's important to you.

Do NOT take Racial Battle Fatigue lightly. It can easily turn into a serious mental health issue such as depression. Set boundaries with Becky. Make your mental health a top priority and seek professional help if you need to.

Don't Waste Your Magic: How will you avoid Racial Battle Fatigue?

_____

_____

_____

_____

_____

"If I didn't define myself for **myself** I would be crunched into other **people's** fantasies for me and **"** eaten alive.

-Audre Lorde

CHAPTER FOUR

Weapons **of**
Whiteness

"White women's **racism** will cut you in the dark and then ask you why
you're bleeding." – Rachael Edwards

So what are these Weapons of Whiteness I've been speaking of? You've probably experienced the emotional violence and Racial Battle Fatigue they inflict upon you, yet you didn't know what to call them. These weapons are centuries old, inherently present in white women (in all white people), and extremely lethal to your emotional and mental wellness. White folks are not born racist; however, they are indoctrinated into white supremacy when they take their first breath. These violent weapons are treacherous and have been the cause of many black and brown women's emotional stress, mental fatigue, and sometimes the taking of their own lives. Sisters, please don't take these weapons as innocent mistakes! They are lethal to your livelihood. I briefly talked about *Weapons of Whiteness* in Chapter 1 and in my book *White Spaces Missing Faces*. Here's an excerpt from that book that describes the Weapons of Whiteness:

Wherever there are white women, there is racism. Where there is racism, there is toxic white feminism. Toxic white feminism ranges from a subtle dismissive assault to a grandiose racist slap in the face. In every space and place where white women exist, women of color who enter these spaces are sure to experience the racist wrath of *Weapons of Whiteness;* therefore and rightfully so, women of color do NOT trust white women.

Engaging in relationships with white women is a psychological risk for many women of color, and "good" white women are the *most* deceptively dangerous. Women of color have doubtful disdain, cautious optimism and deep skepticism about white women, because for centuries, white women have ignored our plight and exploited our experiences for their own edification, entertainment and evolution.

White women have always been intrigued by our skin tone, curious about our hair and often intimidated by our presence and voice. Their poisonous assumptions, racial stereotypes and implicit biases have determined if we are allowed in *their* white space, how far we climb, and if we climb at all. In white women spaces, white women are the equivalent to what they despise, white male patriarchy. In their own solipsistic oblivion, the very oppressive power white women fight against is raging inside of them. White women fight against white male patriarchy and women of color fight to resist White Toxic Feminism.

White women are willful instigators, spectators and perpetrators of our pain. Disingenuous relationships riddled with deception, distrust, doubt and danger has been the nature of our relationships with white women since our first encounter with them. From our earliest memories and throughout our adult years, our value has been examined and analyzed through the proverbial and problematic *White Gaze*; the piercing, skeptical eye of white folks questioning and determining whether people of color are worthy of their time and if they are palatable to their psychological palate.

Yes. All white women are dangerous. Especially in the dominion of their White Spaces. You may be saying, "*No, Catrice, not all white women.*" Yes, ALL white women! Every single one of them belong to the good ole girl's white supremacy club, have been infected with the dis-ease of racism and indoctrinated with *Weapons of Whiteness*. Weapons they've learned from their mothers, aunts and grandmothers on how to engage with and dominate women of color into submission and oppression. White women have devalued our existence, demoralized our history and continue to sharpen their weapons of violation and oppression.

White women historically and collectively have never been our sisters. White women have yet to unanimously express overwhelming sadness or anger about the state of black and brown women's lives. White women have yet to fight for justice and the liberation of black and brown women's lives. Instead, we, women of color are reminded of the white woman's intrinsic deficiency of empathy for our pain and plight.

Will there ever be a time when white women unanimously express overwhelming despair and outrage about the state of black and brown women's lives? Will there ever be a time where collectively white women risk their lives and put their resources on the line to stand up for black and brown women?

Will white women ever create spaces where they refuse to attack, abuse and oppress women of color? Is it possible? Any of it?

Is it possible for white women to cure themselves from the dis-ease of racism? Will white women finally deal with their toxic white feminism and lay down their Weapons of Whiteness to truly be our sisters? Will there ever be a time when women of color can easily, genuinely and consistently trust white women? I don't know. It hasn't happened for centuries, and I'm not sure it can happen now. I do know that NOW is the time for white women to stop being so damn fragile and afraid and do what's right.

Women of color have centuries of legitimate reasons to NOT trust white women: in personal relationships, on the job and online. Racism and White Feminism are paramount to why women of color do NOT attend, participate, thrive or stay in white spaces. White spaces are toxic breeding grounds for racial interpersonal violence under the guise of "feminism" and women's empowerment.

White toxic feminism is full of Weapons of Whiteness: the conscious and unconscious behaviors and words lethally used to deny your existence, stifle your spirit, silence your voice, and paralyze your progress. White women learn and acquire this assaultive arsenal of weapons, which is directly and vicariously taught by white mothers, grandmothers, sisters, and aunts. White women have been recklessly and unapologetically discharging these weapons against black and brown women for centuries. In the table below, I list the top twenty-one weapons and give a brief description of each one. I'll be expanding on these weapons throughout the book.

Weapon of Whiteness Racism = White Supremacy	Catriceology Definition
1. White Silence	When white women hide behind their White Privilege to refuse to speak up about racism.

2. White Fragility	When white women are unable to engage in real conversations about racism without becoming emotionally discombobulated, lashing out, and/or withdrawing.
3. White Innocence	When white women hide behind their White Privilege to avoid having to acknowledge, understand, and/or be knowledgeable about racism and its effects.
4. White Denial	When white women refuse to admit their own racism and/or acknowledge the systemic, structural racism and oppression of white supremacy.
5. White Entitlement or Centering	When white women consume time, space, and conversations; in other words, when they make themselves the center of attention. Also, when they expect to be taught, considered, and forgiven.
6. White Tears	When white women cry during discussions about racism, or when they express that they feel attacked, shamed, and/or hurt when their racism is pointed out or confronted.
7. White Superiority/Authority	When white women use their whiteness to dominate women of color: speaking for and over, interrupting, taking up space, cutting in line, and dismissing their presence.

8. White Derailment	When during conversations about race and racism, white women shift the focus, insert a different topic, and/or minimize, justify, and/or rationalize racism.
9. Whitesplaining	When white women attempt to educate black and brown women on racism, oppression, and white supremacy.
10. White Spirit-splaining	When white women use New Age and spiritual theories, concepts, and language to dismiss, minimize, and derail conversations about racism.
11. White Guilt and Shame	When white women become consumed and paralyzed by guilt and shame, and then project it onto black and brown women by shifting the blame.
12. White Collusion	When white women willingly and/or unknowingly co-conspire with white supremacy and racism at the expense of black and brown people.
13. White Saviorism	When white women demonstrate performative allyship behavior for the sake of being seen as the heroes and/or as showing pity.

14. White Gaslighting	When white women are abusers who silence, scare, and emotionally paralyze their victims. Gaslighting is a highly manipulative and violent act.
15. White Tone Policing or Dominance	When white women tell black and brown women how and when to speak about racism, oppression, and white supremacy.
16. White Righteousness	When white women judge people of color based on what is "white right," and demand right or wrong responses from POC through the use of White Interrogation. These kinds of folks are more interested in being right (perfectionist) in their Allyship than being effective.
17. White Interrogation	When white women ask black and brown people too many emotionally laborious DAMN questions and expect answers.
18. White Feminism	When white women claim they support and advocate for ALL women, yet fail to (or refuse to) center, prioritize, and amplify women of color and their needs and challenges.

19. White Privilege	When white women have the luxury of not having to think about, talk about, or experience racism. It is the unearned safety, access, permission, credibility, inclusion, preference, approval, and protection they possess only because they were born white.
20. White Performative Apology	When white women have been called out, called forward, called in, and/or critiqued on the use of a Weapon of Whiteness, and then they publicly apologize to look good, yet withdraw or lash out behind the scenes.
21. White Intellectualizing	When white women fail to express empathy for the racism black and brown people experience, and instead respond from a cognitive and intellectual space.

Have you experienced the wicked wrath of these weapons? Have your engagements with white women been laborious, overwhelming, frustrating, and maddening? Have white women said or done things to harm you, but you really couldn't put your finger on what was happening to you? You're not imagining this violence. My Sister, you've had Weapons of Whiteness drawn on you. The treachery of white women varies among individuals, but it's always violent. When white women feel threatened, or are afraid and/or upset with women (people) of color, their weapons are always lethal.

I'm sure you've heard the expression "Hell hath no fury like a woman scorned." Well, a white woman scorned has the fury, violence, and volatility of Hurricane Katrina. White women on the defense are like a destructive category five hurricane: unpredictable, vicious, and ferocious. Why do white women behave this way? Because *they* can, and because centuries of passed down, indoctrinated White Superiority has given them undisputed permission to be violent while remaining protected by the cloak of white supremacy. When I work with white women on uprooting and dismantling their racism, I tell them that they walk around in full riot gear every day. White supremacy has given them every weapon they possess, and given them permission to use them with no regard to our humanity, yet they expect and demand to be safe and protected from any retribution they may face as a result of discharging their weapons.

Has there ever been a time in history when white women weren't encouraged to be violent against women of color? There have been no real collective consequences for white women who did nothing to cease the annihilation of Native and Indigenous people or who participated in the intentional destruction of Native people and their culture. There have been no collective consequences for white women who bought, sold, raped, murdered, and dehumanized black men and women. Never *ever* has there been a time in history when white women have been held accountable for their sociopathic crimes against black and brown humanity. And this is exactly why white women continue to unload their fatal arsenal of weapons onto black, brown, Native, and Indigenous men and women.

What's important for you to know is that each and every one of their weapons is rooted in White Superiority. Simply put, white women believe they are better than black, brown, Native, and Indigenous women. It doesn't matter if they are a part of the LGBTQIA+ community. It doesn't matter if they grew up in the hood, or if they date black and brown men or women. It doesn't matter if they have biracial or multiracial children. It doesn't matter if they are poor, working class, Democrat, feminist, or a so-called "Ally." White women truly believe they are superior and are thus entitled to say and do whatever they want to women of color. With no collective consequences for their behaviors and protection under the cloak of white supremacy, they will continue to discharge deadly weapons at will.

Are you still wondering why? Do you think there is more to this violence than skin color? If you said yes, you are correct. As a Licensed Mental Health Practitioner (LMHP), Licensed Professional Counselor (LPC), and doctoral student in Psychology working on my dissertation related to mental health and racism, I know there absolutely is something more disturbing to this violent behavior. For the past year, I've been informally researching possible reasons why white folks (white women in particular) treat people of color with such disdain, and why they dismiss their lived racial experiences. Although the search continues, I've already made some conclusions. The following is a summary of what I wrote about the pathology and toxicity of racism in my book White Spaces Missing Faces:

RACISM IS TOXIC and white people who live inside this racist mental space are willfully caught in an illusion that has robbed them of their true identity, has caused a deep, apathetic disassociation from humanity, and has altered their sense of reality. You may think this is an exaggeration, but if you examine racism closely you'll see it. The racism I'm referring to is your *every day* racism, and I'm not talking about the burning crosses and radical Nazi behavior racism; I'm talking about good ole, regular "good white folks" racism. **Racism. How do we define it?** The standard dictionary definition does the word no justice and leaves too much grey area.

"Racism refers to a variety of practices, beliefs, social relations, and phenomena that work to reproduce a racial hierarchy and social structure that yield superiority, power, and privilege for some, and discrimination and oppression for others. Racism takes representational, ideological, discursive, interactional, institutional, structural, and systemic forms. But despite its form, at its core, racism exists when ideas and assumptions about racial categories are used to justify and reproduce a racial hierarchy and racially structured society that unjustly limits access to resources, rights, and privileges on the basis of race. Racism also occurs when this kind of unjust social structure is produced by the failure to account for race and its historic and contemporary roles in society. By this sociological definition, racism is about much more than race-based prejudice—it exists as an imbalance in power and social status is generated by how we understand and act upon race." -- Cole, N.L. (July 24, 2017). "The Definition of Racism." Retrieved from www.thoughtco.com/racism-definition-3026511.

This definition illuminates racism on the macro-level, but does not allow white people to clearly acknowledge and see how racism on a micro-level is just as lethal and oppressive. "Good" white people don't believe they are racist because the definition above depicts the image of racism they have in their mind. They believe they are NOT racist because they don't burn flags, use racial slurs or exhibit blatant racist behavior. Racism is NOT fixed, but rather a fluid, often invisible and subtle array of micro thoughts and behaviors that cause emotional harm to people of color also known as Microaggressions.

"Racial microaggressions are brief and commonplace daily verbal, behavioral, or environmental indignities, whether intentional or unintentional, that communicate hostile, derogatory, or negative racial slights and insults toward people of color. Perpetrators of microaggressions are often unaware that they engage in such communications when they interact with racial/ethnic minorities."
–Dr. Derald Wing Sue

Hostile. Derogatory. Negative Insults. The ways in which "good" white folks engage with people of color every day. There's a BIG psychological disconnect between the belief that one is good yet he or she demonstrates hostile, derogatory, assaultive behavior frequently on a daily basis. How does this happen? Racism and being a part of the institutionalized system of white supremacy (which all white people fit into including the "good ones") has strong psychological characteristics of Narcissism. According to current literature on Narcissism and the medical definition of *Narcissistic Personality Disorder*, here are a few behaviors of those who exhibit characteristics of and/or are diagnosed with this mental health disorder according to the DSM IV [Diagnostic and Statistical Manual of Mental Health Disorders Fourth Edition].

How Narcissism and Racism are Similar

- Narcissists dominate conversations (refuse to listen to people of color).

- Narcissists believe they have superior knowledge (white entitlement and whitesplaning).

- Narcissists believe they deserve special treatment (white entitlement).

- Narcissists believe they are special or different than others ("not me, I'm a good white person").

- Narcissists have a strong desire to hold on to a perceived self-image (white denial).

- Narcissists have trouble accepting even the smallest criticism and see it as a personal attack (white fragility).

- Narcissists have a strong sense of not wanting to be held accountable for mistakes and the tendency to blame others (defense and derailment tactics due to white fragility).

- Narcissists lack empathy (often don't believe the stories of people of color).

- Narcissists expect others to revolve around their needs (white centeredness), and are manipulative (white tears).

If I stop here, it's clear racism has pulled a doozy of a mental scheme on white folks. Narcissistic Personality Disorder is one of the top personality disorders classified in the *Diagnostic and Statistical Manual of Mental Disorders* (DSM IV) and one of the most difficult to treat. This manual is used by therapists, psychiatrists and psychologists to diagnose and treat their patients/clients. In my practice as a Licensed Mental Health Practitioner and Licensed Professional Counselor, I have personally engaged with and counseled people with this diagnosis and it is strikingly similar to engaging with a white Antagonist.

White Antagonists, when discussing race and racism show up exactly like those diagnosed with Narcissistic Personality Disorder:

- They think they know more about racism than people of color.

- They refuse to believe the validity of people of color's lived racial experiences

- They exhaust themselves trying to prove they are different and that they're a good white person.

- They expect people of color to talk nicely to them about racism and to NOT call them out.

- They are easily offended when people of color question or challenge their white privilege.

- They often have emotional meltdowns, instead of taking responsibility
for their lack of knowledge and/ or oppressive behaviors.

- They blame people color by calling them negative, angry, and divisive.

- They try to derail racism conversations by shifting the focus on to topics that have nothing to do with racism.

- They want to be at the center of the conversation when discussing racism and expect people of color to cater to their white fragility and white tears.

Pretty narcissistic wouldn't you say? You can't win with a Narcissist so don't even try. They know everything and refuse to listen. The same is true for the Antagonist. It is a complete waste of time trying to have race talks or discuss racism with Antagonists and you're sure to be mentally antagonized and emotionally depleted. Racism and racist behavior takes white folks down the path of Cognitive Dissonance.

Cognitive Dissonance: is the state of having simultaneous, inconsistent thoughts, beliefs, or attitudes, especially as relating to behavioral decisions and attitude change: "Cognitive Dissonance is a communication theory that was published by Leon Festinger in 1957, a theory that changed the way in which social psychology was to look at human decision-making and behaviour." —de Canonville, C. L. (2017). "The place of 'Cognitive Dissonance' in Narcissistic Victim Syndrome." Retrieved from http://narcissisticbehavior. net/the-place-of-cognitive-dissonance-in-narcissistic-victim-syndrome/.

The majority of white folks *know* racism is wrong and many would disagree with it. However, those same good folks don't see *themselves* as racist and or perpetrators of racism. Here's where the dissonance comes into play. How can white folks on one hand KNOW racism exists and that it's wrong, yet, believe they are NOT contributors or perpetrators of it? These two thoughts are simultaneously consistent in the minds of white folks, especially those who deem themselves good Christian white folks. This conflict of beliefs is closely connected to narcissism and the belief that they are "*different than other white folks and special.*"

This dissonance creates an uncomfortable reality for many white folks. Why? Because when they are confronted with the idea or accusation they are racist or participating in racism, internal conflict arises that forces them to acknowledge that their behaviors have hurt others (people of color) despite their moral declarations of being good, thus contradicting their values and beliefs. When exposed to this startling discomfort they will do one of two things:

1. ***Hold on to their beliefs despite the glaring data presented that contradicts their beliefs*** (*I'm a good person. I can't possibly be racist*).

2. See the contradiction and work to modify their thoughts and beliefs to create consistency in thoughts and behaviors *(I have racial biases. I am racist. I've done racist things. I will work to unlearn my racial biases. I benefit from racism and how can I use my power and privilege to be an Ally for racial injustice?)*

The **Antagonist** (aka Narcissist) will hold on for dear life and traumatize people of color in the process of fighting to maintain their skewed sense of *equilibrium;* because you know a narcissist can never be wrong, right? The three most common reactions and actions to maintain equilibrium for Antagonists are to **deny, defend and divert**; this is especially true when engaging in discussions about race and racism. They will deny they are racist, defend their "good white person" status and/or attempt to derail (divert) the conversation by shifting the focus on to a non-related topic, accuse people of color for being divisive, and an uneducated Antagonist will proclaim that reverse racism (there's no such thing) is occurring.

And the most narcissistic Antagonists will become emotionally distraught, cry and run away to manipulate you into believing it's **your** fault they feel shame and or guilt (Gaslighting). Whew!... Engaging with Antagonists in conversations about race is emotionally taxing, physically draining and the worst part is, they don't even realize how toxic their thoughts and beliefs are not only to people of color, but themselves.

The dissonance within them creates internalized stress, conflict, anxiety and mental chaos which are detrimental to *their* health and well-being. The energy exerted in order to keep up the *"I'm a good person"* facade has to be emotionally and spiritually daunting. The drastic need to avoid the truth and fear of facing one's implicit racial biases is literally too much to bear for white people. They don't want to be exposed as racist. All of this is extremely toxic and I can only imagine what it does to their souls. Better yet, I don't have to imagine. Being on the receiving end of this antagonistic, racist toxicity is far worse and emotionally oppressive.

Why would someone cling to this mindset, beliefs and behaviors? Wouldn't it make sense to address this apathetic **disconnect from humanity** and liberate themselves from the toxicity of racism? But you see, many white people don't see it this way. Most white people who choose to step up and be a voice against racism truly believe they are "white saviors" saving people of color from those "racists" *out there*. In fact, White Savior Syndrome is a part of racism. **White people don't see the racism that lives within them.** They don't see they are **dying inside** too and that they are inadvertently affected and infected by the *dis-ease* **of racism** as a result of being an indoctrinated member of the institution of white supremacy.

Racism and white supremacy has done one hell of a number on white folks and they don't even know it (or pretend they don't know). Like deadly carbon monoxide, racism has seeped into every fiber of their being and they don't know it's about to kill them. That's deep and disturbing! Yet many white people cling to their implicit biases, their cognitive dissonance and narcissism to remain *"a good white person"* all while internally suffering from the very dis-ease they refuse to address, but know exists. White Fragility is vehemently violent! The silence, denial, derailment, arguing, failing to listen and lack of empathy expressed when people of color are expressing real life racial trauma causes secondary trauma. This coupled with the *expectation* of people of color to "teach them or educate them" is emotional insult, riddled with white entitlement and emotional abuse. I'm a firm believer that racism is abuse even when it's "unintentional."

White folks will abuse people of color with racial microaggressions, get emotional and upset because they are called out, and then say *"Well how am I supposed to learn if you don't teach me?"* Essentially, they're saying *"let me keep abusing you while you teach me how not to."* There is something psychologically and fundamentally wrong with that, but white folks do this every day and think nothing of it. They are completely apathetic about the lived experiences of people of color and often contribute to their pain and oppression.

So...let's bring this full circle. When white people refuse to acknowledge and admit to racism and their active or passive participation in it, essentially they are denying their role in the emotional abuse, trauma and oppression of people of color. When white people engage in race talks with people of color as an Antagonist it's not only emotionally abusive and mentally exhausting it's **Gaslighting**. Gaslighting is a manipulative, emotionally abusive tactic used by abusers to make their victims doubt their reality and second guess the truth of their lived experiences. Furthermore, the narcissistic behavior is loaded with emotionally abusive and manipulative tactics that cause people of color more frustration, anger, pain and mental trauma. And to seal this toxic deal, cognitive dissonance allows them to fight to resist what's glaringly obvious to maintain their safe space of *"I'm a good person"* while abusing the hell out of people of color and preserving their **entitlement** to remain safe.

- Does that really sound like a "good" person to you?

- Does a good person deny someone's painful truth to stay emotionally safe?

- Does a good person lie about their participation in one's trauma?

- Does a good person demand your silence when you speak up about your abuse?

- Does a good person argue with you when you're begging to be heard or trying to survive?

- Does a good person watch you being abused and say absolutely nothing?

- Does a good person mentally and emotionally abuse other people?

Let me be crystal clear. While white folks are inherently a part of the American system of white supremacy and institutionalized racism, this does NOT justify or excuse racist behavior whether intentional or unintentional. There is no excuse for emotionally, mentally, or physically abusing anyone. A lot of white folks want to be safe when talking about race and racism. Ironically, the victims of racism are NEVER safe from racism; not even in a conversation about it. Isn't it bizarre that white folks want to be safe during race talks, yet it's highly probable (unless they've done some significant anti-racism work) people of color will be abused by them during the engagement? This expectation of safety is diabolical. It says, "Keep me safe while I abuse you." Racism is toxic and White Fragility is violent. It's a lose/lose situation... White people who refuse to wake up to these truths will spend the rest of their lives as an abuser and die from the carbon monoxide of racism.

My Sister, if I have not yet made the definition and effects of Beckyism crystal clear, everything you've just read encompasses Becky, her Beckery, and her virulent disease of Beckyism. When I say white women are armed and dangerous, I'm serious. Whether their Weapons of Whiteness are discharged intentionally or unintentionally does NOT minimize or excuse the pain, abuse, and trauma you experience. You matter. Your emotional and mental wellness matters. You can no longer afford to waste your magic on the Becky! Now that you understand the reality and lethality of dealing with White Woman Violence, get ready to learn how to Defy the Beckery!

Cracking the BECKY Code Clues

Don't fall for the "good white woman" façade. All white women are Beckys.

Learn how to spot gaslighting now. Doing so will help prevent unnecessary stress and will signal you to use your WIN strategy, which I will be sharing with you in Chapter 7.

When white women draw Weapons of Whiteness against you, call them out on their violence and refuse to let them steal your joy.

Don't Waste Your Magic: What weapons has Becky used to harm you?

_____

_____

_____

_____

_____

_____

_____

_____

"Whatever is bringing you down, get rid of it. Because you'll find that when you're **free...** your true self comes out.**"**

-Tina Turner

CHAPTER FIVE
Defying **the** Beckery

"In a world that directly and indirectly tells Women of Color they are not worthy, qualified, invited, beautiful, or valued, we must deny EVERY restriction, affliction, prediction, and depiction that causes us to stay captive, be unhealed, doubt our destiny, and fail to embrace our beauty."
– Catrice M. Jackson

"Oh my God, Becky, look at her butt!" Ugh! Becky has been around forever, but was first identified by her infamous name in Sir Mix-A-Lot's hit song "Baby Got Back" in 1992. That's when the mainstream media could finally put face and name to this white woman's clueless but violent persona. The Becky from the 1990s is the same Becky of millennia. Her self-absorbed, oppressive roots haven't changed, but now she produces more abusive fruit under the deceptive labels of *feminism, liberal,* and *progressive.* Yes, even those white women who claim to be intersectional feminists are Becky, because if she is NOT centering the voices of black, brown, Native, and Indigenous people, *especially* black women and femmes, then she is NOT intersectional and is indeed a Becky!

I've been dealing with some vile variation of Becky and her damn Beckery for as long as I can remember, and I imagine you have too. So what is this damn Beckery? The short answer is that Beckery is the White Woman Violence I've been talking about throughout this book. Another answer is:

> *Beckery* is the oblivious, obnoxious, and oppressive way in which white women view the world through their white supremacist lenses that leads to invalidating, insulting, and assaulting people (especially women) of color with violent Weapons of Whiteness. Beckery is intentional, insidious, and invasive. Some Beckys know exactly what they're doing, while others act out of willful ignorance on the daily. Both ways of showing up invade your space, peace, and joy. Beckery aims to do one of four things to people of color and their lived racial experiences: **Deny, Defend, Derail,** and **Destroy.**

Catrice Jackson • 55

Let's talk about the deadliness of denial. Some people say denial of racism is the *new* racism. I say denial is one of the oldest deadly weapons used by white people to silence your truth, and to avoid taking responsibility for their own racism and white supremacy. White Denial is intellectual disassociation; it's a form of cognitive dissonance from the reality of past and present white supremacist structures and systems that marginalize, paralyze, and oppress people of color.

Denial is dismissive apathy that disregards the painful truth about the violence and oppression of people of color. The value placed on white people's feelings and White Comfort is, and has been, more important than the lived racial experiences of black, brown, Native, and Indigenous people. When white people deny racism, white supremacy, and White Privilege, their sole intent is to shut you up and shift the blame for your experiences and problems onto you.

Denial is deadly: it causes you to question your own truth, and to second-guess your pain. It's purposely used to strangle your story. White people deny racism and white supremacy to distance themselves from the unearned privileges and benefits they reap from being white. Denial helps them avoid having to admit they are an active participant in the complicity of crimes against black, brown, Native, and Indigenous humanity. White folks KNOW that racism and white supremacy is horrible and evil, but the fact that they benefit socially from racism and white supremacy by being white is too painful to bear. Therefore, their denial of your truth about racist experiences keeps them safe, comfortable, and unaccountable.

Denial is a psychological defense mechanism we all use to help keep us safe. When white folks are called out on their racism or asked to examine the truth about societal racism, they will defend themselves into exhaustion to avoid seeing the treachery of whiteness. Beckys will DEFEND themselves, and their racist friends, family, and colleagues to the ends of the Earth because they are guilty by association. In their defense of horrendous crimes committed against people of color, Becky will project the problem back on to you, blame you for your pain, and DENY that she caused it. When a white woman is in defense mode, she has two goals in mind: to DERAIL the conversation about racism and, to DESTROY your emotional well-being with her Weapons of Whiteness.

Beckery is violently exhausting and it will *invalidate your truth, insult your intelligence, and assault your spirit*. Beckery will emotionally kill you unless you learn how to DEFY THE BECKERY with Deliberate Defiance. *Deliberate Defiance* is the act of intentional resistance and bold disobedience in response to *all* the spoken and insidious forms of racism you deal with on a daily basis. After all, one of the central aims of racism is to maintain control over black and brown bodies and minds. Racism is one of the master's (white supremacy's) tools intentionally used to silence, paralyze, and marginalize black, brown, Native, and Indigenous people. It's essential that you know how to take back and maintain your emotional control when dealing with Becky and her white weapons.

Beckys are emotional vampires; don't let them engulf your precious energy! DON'T WASTE YOUR MAGIC! By *magic,* I mean your spirit and your joy. By *magic,* I mean the stride in your step, the sparkle in your eye, and the power in which you move around in the world. By *magic,* I mean your genius, the brilliance in your melanin, and the magnificence of your being. By *magic,* I mean your ingenuity, your divinity, and your integrity. By *magic,* I mean your strength, power, and resiliency. You *are* magic in all of your gigantic gloriousness! But you are not just magical, you are also **real** my Sister: a real human being with feelings that matter. You matter so much that you must make YOU the number one priority, so that you not only survive, but thrive within WHITE society.

White women secretly covet your magic. Many of them are awakening to the truth that they fell for the fool's gold of the *perceived* global racial majority. Black, brown, Native, and Indigenous people are the *true* global majority. White women are extremely malnourished beings. They thirst and hunger for realness, roots, culture, and identity. They don't know who they are, so they take on identities such as goddess, priestess, guru, bombshell, shaman, warrior queen, and witch, and all of their other made-up, self-soothing crap to feel alive. They're starving. They're starving for connectedness because they're disconnected from humanity, especially black and brown humanity. This is why they have no reservations about carnivorously consuming black, brown, Native, and Indigenous cultures without restriction, and why they get angry and cry when you question the blood on their hands and the bones in their backyard. This is how they consume YOUR magic!

White women especially ravage black women's culture. The 1990s Beckys from the beginning of this chapter, went from "oh my God, look at her butt" to the thirty-day squat challenge to firm up their butts. Those same Beckys who called black women "Ghetto" back in the day now gobble up every damn bit of AAVE (African American Vernacular English) they can to sound cool and to perpetrate the fraud of being *woke*! White women slither into your presence and call you "Sistah" while slaying you with Weapons of Whiteness in the same breath. From the time black women were savagely and unwillingly brought to America, white women have despised us while secretly admiring our strength, strength we had to gain to survive their wrath. After beating us down for centuries, the Beckys of today covet and hunger for that same strength often to the extreme of fetishization... remember Rachel from Chapter 2? Ugh!

Every obstacle, barrier, and challenge you've experienced as a result of your melanin makes you magical. To possess magic means to have extraordinary power or influence, seemingly from a supernatural force. God knows that after all you've been through in your life, and for all the times you've experienced and survived racism, you, my Sister, possess a magical and extraordinary supernatural power that keeps you alive and thriving. It's supernatural to simply live, breath, and exist in black and brown skin in this world. It takes extraordinary strength to stand in your power in a society that directly and indirectly tells you that you are not worthy, qualified, invited, beautiful, valued, or loved. Because you exist, resist, persist, survive, and thrive, YOU ARE MAGIC!

> Your magic will help you deny EVERY restriction, affliction, prediction, and depiction that causes you to stay captive, be unhealed, doubt your destiny, and fail to embrace your power and beauty! You are significant! You matter! It's time to harness and activate your magic! Remember that White Woman Violence is meant to deny your truth, defend racism, derail the real problem of white supremacy, and destroy your joy.

Sister… you're not magic for nothing! You too have weapons to use when Becky comes for you! Yes, Girlfriend, you have *Weapons for Winning* the war of Beckyism. When Becky comes to Deny, Defend, Derail, and Destroy, you can whip out the *Four D's for Defying the Beckery*. Unlike Becky's attempt to cause harm with her weapons, Weapons for Winning are specifically designed to deflect her destruction, protect your power, and amplify your joy. I know Becky is exhausting as hell, but it's time to stop letting her Beckery get the best of you. Becky ain't going anywhere. In one way or another, you'll have to deal with her, so you might as well learn how to defy her deadly weapons.

Audre Lorde says, "Your silence will not protect you." She's right. There have been days when Becky and other white folks have used their weapons against me and I was just too tired to fight back, days when I've already had thousands of white weapons used against me. There have been times when Becky's weapons have caught me off guard and left me speechless. And in all of those moments of emotional attack, one thing is for sure: my silence did NOT protect me. Choosing to ignore Weapons of Whiteness may temporarily shield you, and may be the best option in some cases, but perpetual silence will not only NOT protect you, it will kill you emotionally.

Silence is the voice of complicity. Remember the Zora Neale Hurston quote from Chapter 2? She said, "If you are silent about your pain, they will kill you and say you enjoyed it." Sisters… you must no longer be silent about your pain and complicit in the murdering of your soul. Racial oppression is intentional. It and its perpetrators are purposely trying to kill your spirit so you won't fight for justice, equity, equality, and liberation. White people are counting on YOU to stay silent about white supremacy, racism, and your pain, because your silence feeds the beast of white supremacy that seeks to kill you. They are betting that you will continue to carry the burden of oppression until it exhausts the life out of you. White folks will continue to DENY your truth, and so you must DARE to speak even when you're tired and afraid.

DARING to speak is one of the Weapons for Winning. When white women deny your truth, and attempt to silence your voice, you must declare to be heard. Of course your declaration must come after discernment.

Not every battle is worth fighting. If you fight every Becky who denies your truth, you will not win, and I don't mean "win" in the literal sense. You don't have enough magic to defy every Becky, and that's not what your magic is ultimately for. The win I want you to achieve is winning in your life in every way imaginable and unimaginable! I have a strategy to help you decrease Racial Battle Fatigue and win, my friend! And here it is!

Weapons for Winning and Amplifying Your Joy

1. **DARE to Speak**: When white women DENY your truth, stories, and experiences, DARE to speak and call them out on their violations and violence. Of course, you must DISCERN whether this is a battle you're willing to engage in or not. If you decide that it isn't, remember that your silence will not protect you. If you fail to address Becky's violence, she is likely to violate you again. Iyanla Vanzant says, *"We must call a thing a thing."* This means you must identify and name racism for what it is by calling it out explicitly as white supremacy.

2. **DISOBEY the Expectations**: When white women DEFEND their racism, they *expect* you to stay silent and to accept their manipulative, defensive rationale. They *expect* you to understand their "mistake." They *expect* you to talk nicely to them about your pain while they cause it. They *expect* you to pull them to the side and not call them out publicly. They *expect* you to NOT shame them. They *expect* you to forgive them for their violence. They *expect* you to watch your tone and to not be angry. They *expect* you to explain or teach them about racism. DISOBEY ALL OF THOSE EXPECTATIONS!
   - DO NOT let them take your kindness for weakness.
   - DO NOT subdue your tone and your voice. Remember what Zora says!
   - DO NOT feel the need to talk privately about their racism. They will abuse you behind closed doors.

- DO NOT let them manipulate you with declarations of shame and their White Tears.
- You DO NOT have to forgive their violence.
- DO NOT waste your magic and emotional energy on educating them.
- Be angry and mad if you want to. You DO NOT need anyone's permission or approval to express your anger. (Don't stay angry, however, because doing so hurts only you).
- DO NOT FOLLOW THEIR RULES OF ENGAGEMENT. DISOBEY EVERY DAMN TIME! For centuries, white folks have had the expectation that black and brown folks would follow their white rules and expectations. You don't have to!

3. **DISCONTINUE the Dialogue**: When white women try to DERAIL the conversation about racism, know that this is an intentional tactic used to avoid looking at their own racism. White folks get extremely uncomfortable when talking about racism, and they will try to create an intellectual and emotional distraction to avoid dealing with their passive or active role in racism and white supremacy. Instead of following them into the violent white abyss, call out their attempt to derail the conversation. At this point, Becky has made it clear that she does not want to hear your truth or to stop her racial violence. DETACH. It's time to DISCONTINUE dialoguing with her. This is not a battle you want to try to win. It's at this point that we give away our precious energy and power to antagonistic white women who do not want to change. Walk away. You do not have to prove your humanity to them. They are NOT worth the agony.

4. **DETOX and Delight**: When white women try to DESTROY your joy, say, *"Nah, not today, Becky!"* On some days, it is worth the fight to go into battle with Becky. But I want to encourage you to choose a different, more nourishing option instead on most days. When the need arises, then dare to speak, disobey the expectations,

discontinue the dialogue, and demand to be heard and respected. And don't forget to maintain your magic by detoxing yourself from the Beckyism. You are here for a very special reason and a divine purpose. Don't let Becky hijack your destiny! Taking care of yourself and making YOU priority number one is essential. I'll share more on how to detox yourself from the Beckery and how to delight in your magnificent magic in upcoming chapters.

Weapons of Whiteness are real. You've been experiencing their wrath all of your life and now you have the words to describe the assault. It doesn't matter if white women know they have these weapons and that they harm women of color or not. Weapons of Whiteness will always deny your truth, defend racism, derail conversations about racism, and destroy your joy. But when Becky comes for you, you can certainly come for her.

Remember that you now have Weapons for Winning, the *Four D's for Defying the Beckery:* Dare, Disobey, Discontinue, and Detox. Using them is your right. You don't need permission to protect and defend your humanity. You can choose to say, "Nah, Becky, not today," and instead preserve your emotional energy. Whatever you choose, just know that you don't have to put up with Becky and you CAN defy her Beckery!

Cracking the BECKY Code Clues

Becky is a narcissist and she does not respond to coddling and empathy. You must be firm and unapologetic with her. Set strong boundaries and hold her accountable for her behavior.

Don't be fooled by *Wanna-Be-Black Becky*. She is not as "woke" as she may seem. Don't get too comfortable around her. She is one of the most violent Beckys of all.

Remember that Becky will try to manipulate you by crying White Tears.

Do not fall for this trick. Her tears are a deceptive tool to center herself and silence you.

Don't Waste Your Magic: How will you defy the Beckery?

_____

_____

_____

_____

_____

_____

_____

_____

_____

_____

_____

_____

_____

_____

_____

"The most common **way** people **give** up their **power** is by thinking they don't have **any."**

-Alice Walker

CHAPTER SIX
Cracking the Becky Code

"I will not have my life narrowed down. I will not bow down to somebody else's whim or to someone else's ignorance." – Bell Hooks

---

To successfully defy Becky with your Weapons for Winning, you must know Becky and all of her motives. In other words, you must crack her code. The truth is (and I say this with a bit of skepticism), Becky doesn't know herself. For the most part, I truly believe that Becky knows what she is doing when she draws her weapons on you. However, after hosting several in-person anti-racism workshops around the country, as well as online courses designed to teach white women how to lay down their weapons, my skepticism is valid.

I realize just how oblivious white women are to the severity, depth, and breadth of the toxic white supremacy waters they swim in daily. They've been swimming in this societal cesspool of privilege, unearned power, and apathy all of their lives. Like fish, if you ask them to define water (white supremacy), they can tell you only that water is wet. In other words, white women know what white supremacy is on a surface level, but they are clueless about just how entrenched and pervasive it is in their lives.

While this may be true for many white women, I do NOT excuse the willful ignorance shown by *any* of them. On rare occasions I can offer a tad bit of grace; otherwise, I have zero tolerance for White Woman Violence. I know Becky better than she knows herself, and so do you. We've had to deal with Becky all of our lives, while she chooses whether, when, where, and how long she will deal with us. That's right; white women tolerate us. We are a disposable option to them. We are an extracurricular activity they can choose to engage in or not. White women don't need us to survive, and they know it. And quite frankly, white women collectively don't give a damn about black, brown, Native, and Indigenous women. Instead, they have shown us:

Wrath.

Weapons.

Riot gear.

Sounds like a war, doesn't it? It is. It's an emotional war and a spiritual battle when we have to deal with Becky and her Beckery. (Remember Racial Battle Fatigue?) And you don't win a war without knowing who you're up against, nor without a strategy or a plan. If you've engaged with one white woman, you've engaged with them all. Sure, white women have different features, characteristics, values, and beliefs. And some of them are folks you may want to be in relationship with. Yet, as it relates to white supremacy and racism, white women clearly have one belief in common: they deeply believe they are superior to other women.

> Every Weapon of Whiteness that white women use is rooted in White Superiority and White Entitlement. If this is not the case, then why has there never been a time in American history when white women have collectively put their lives on the line for women of color?

In other words, why didn't white women stop the genocide of Native people in their own land? Why did they actively participate in the horrendous treatment of Native children who were forced into boarding schools? Why didn't white women say NO to the enslavement and brutality of black people for almost three hundred years? Why did white women build the feminist movement with pillars of racism? Why did black and brown women have to fight and beg white women to be heard and included in the feminist movement? Why didn't white women collectively dismantle the inhumane laws and practices of Jim Crow? I can come to only one logical conclusion when searching for answers to these questions: white women do not give a damn about women of color. With their White Superiority and White Entitlement, white women believe they can treat women of color any way they choose, with no consequences.

White women from centuries ago are the same white women of today. Do not be deceived by the liberal, progressive, pro-feminism Beckys of today. The historical violence of their mothers, grandmothers, and great-grandmothers has been passed down to them. The Beckys of today have been purposely indoctrinated into white supremacy, and have been taught the *White Woman Script* directly and vicariously by the white women in their life. This script, loaded with weapons, is predictable, dangerous, and deadly.

Let's examine this script a little closer. Think about the countless times you've engaged with antagonistic white women regarding racism. Think about all the times they've made comments that cost you emotional labor; in other words, the comments that pissed you off, frustrated you, and/or exhausted you into a surrendering silence. These could be engagements in person, at work, or online. The venue doesn't matter; wherever these conversations take place, they always have the same tone, intent, and outcome. Do you remember the questions I asked about your experience with White Woman Violence in earlier chapters? In addition, you can expect conversations with antagonistic white women to be riddled with the following predictable statements:

- "I don't see color. I just see people."
- "We're all one race; the human race."
- "Why do you have to make everything about race?"
- "You talking about race/racism is just dividing us more."
- "Can I play devil's advocate for a minute?"
- "Well, what about black-on-black crime?"
- "Not all white people are racist."
- "You don't know me. I am far from racist."
- "I understand what it's like to be oppressed. My children are bi/multi-racial."
- "Not all cops are bad."
- "All lives matter."
- "This wouldn't happen if they (people of color) would just listen to the cops."
- "We need unity right now."

- "We don't have all the facts at this point." (When another black man is murdered.)
- "People would probably listen to you if you weren't so angry."
- "I don't have white privilege. I've worked hard for everything I have."
- "You're the one who is racist." (When you call them racist.)

Can you say E.X.H.A.U.S.T.I.N.G! How predictable and typical are these statements? How many times have you heard them? Have you heard statements like these from white women no matter where the conversation takes place? This isn't coincidental or ironic. It's an intentional, perfect design. How is it that white women from all over the country and from different walks of life speak the same scripted, violent language? If you engage in dialogue about racism and white supremacy with antagonistic white women, no matter where in the U.S. they are from, they are sure to use the language from the White Woman Script. These same Beckys will quickly say, "I'm the least racist person you know," right after reciting the top racist statements from the script. You know Becky better than she knows herself, too, which means you're halfway to Cracking the Becky Code.

Let's continue to crack this code so you can defy the Beckery! Here's what you know about the collective Becky:

- There's never been a time in history when Beckys have collectively sacrificed their time, money, energy, resources, or lives for black, brown, Native, and Indigenous women.
- Becky has never been your sister in solidarity.
- Becky doesn't care about your racial struggle.
- Becky is armed and dangerous with Weapons of Whiteness.
- Becky's weapons are rooted in white supremacy and White Entitlement.
- Becky's weapons are intended to deny, defend, derail, and destroy.
- Becky is fragile as hell!

All of this is true for the collective Becky. There may be individual white women who are less violent and oppressive. There may be individual white women who are working to uproot their racism. There may be individual white women who you are willing to call *friend* or *partner*. There may even be individual white women you call *Ally*. However, collectively speaking, the statements above are accurately and painfully true about Becky.

One of the most important facts you need to know about Becky and Beckyism is that not only is her violence rooted in white supremacy and White Entitlement, it is also drenched in White Narcissism. I talked about narcissism and Narcissistic Personality Disorder (NPD) in Chapter 4. As a reminder, NPD is essentially a mental health diagnosis comprised of four main dysfunctional components of personality: self-absorption, authority, superiority, and entitlement. You'll find that those who have NPD exhibit maladaptive personality behaviors: they show up as selfish know-it-alls who think they're better than everyone and are entitled to whatever they want. Sounds like Becky, don't it? White women are narcissistic.

Here's what I know about narcissists. Their interpersonal engagement is completely self-focused, and they suffer from a severe case of BWAM (But What About Me). They exhibit poor insight (the ability to reflect on their behaviors), and have difficulty expressing empathy for others. Narcissists are sensitive to insults, both perceived and real, and easily feel shame if imperfections are pointed out. When you combine all of this with Weapons of Whiteness, white women who are NOT doing their anti-racism work are dangerous to the mental and emotional well-being of women of color. When I speak of White Woman Violence, I truly mean **violence**. Some people believe this is an exaggeration, but if you've experienced the wrath of white women, you know how lethal they can be.

So how do you deal with White Women Narcissists? I've found the best way to deal with them is to understand what drives their behaviors and to NOT allow them to stir me into the Sunken Place (discussed in the next chapter). If you haven't seen the movie **Get Out,** you must. It perfectly captures the insidious and painstakingly real experience of being startled and emotionally transfixed by Weapons of Whiteness. The lead female character in the film is a white woman named Rose. Want to know how she shows up? Go back and read the poem at the beginning of this book, and then see the movie. I wrote my poem before the movie was released, and after I saw the movie, I knew my depiction of The Rose was right.

White Women Narcissists love to be the center of attention. Don't give them a drop of attention, but if you must, call out their racist behavior unapologetically and walk away. If you give any more than that, they will suck you into their arrogant abyss and drain the life out of you. These are the kind of white women you can have no gray area with. They are egomaniacs and thrive on being the focal point. Ignore them completely, or call them out with a firm and unwavering voice. They do not have the ability to pause and evaluate their words and behavior. Their empathy for your oppression is null and void. They will never see or own up to their violence, and they are sure to project the cause of your pain onto you. They are masters at gaslighting the hell out of you while protecting their comfort.

Avoid White Women Narcissists at all costs. Don't give your power away. You cannot win with narcissists. Love yourself enough to refuse to engage. These women have a severe case of cognitive dissonance. In other words, they have two conflicting belief tapes (thoughts and internal messages) playing in their head at the same time. One tape tells them they are a good, loving, and moral person. The other tape tells them that they are superior to non-white people. How can someone be a good AND moral person and think that non-white people are beneath them? It's real easy to put your boot on someone's neck when you don't see and honor their existence.

White women live and breathe in combat boots. They walk through life armed in full riot gear (Weapons of Whiteness), ready at any given moment to discharge violence against you to put their boot on your neck, while claiming (and believing) to be good, loving, and moral people. And when you call out this dissonance, they will deny it, defend themselves, derail the conversation, and destroy your emotional energy. This, my Sister, is White Woman Terrorism in action! Here's something to remember: when white women use their weapons against you, regardless of whether they do so intentionally or unintentionally, it is still painful violence. Of course not all white women will respond to your callout the same way.

Pay close attention to Becky's response to your callout, as it will tell you how far in her anti-racism journey she is and guide your next move. If a white woman responds with shock and anger about your callout, she has not even started the journey. She's going to become highly defensive and discharge her weapons. This is your cue to disengage. On the other hand, if her response is an apology that includes the words "Thank you, I will do better," there's a possibility that you may be able to have some type of dialogue with her. But enter that conversation at your own risk; keep in mind that she is still in full riot gear with weapons locked and loaded. White women who have started the journey expect and often welcome the callout, as they know it's a gift and an opportunity to *know better so they can be better.* If you remain connected to them, the expectation is that the best apology is changed behavior. If she shows up violently with you again, she has learned nothing. Walk away and remember that this is a war you're in.

You deserve better. You are worthy of peace and abundant joy. It doesn't matter whether Becky is Super Becky, Begging Becky, or Know-It-All Becky, she's armed and dangerous. You are armed too, with the insights into Becky that she doesn't even have for herself. That is one of your Weapons for Winning! Trust me. You know Becky better than she knows herself. Don't allow Beckyism to sink you into the Sunken Place. Don't waste your magic! Let's continue to crack The Becky Code.

Cracking the BECKY Code Clues

Listen for the *scripted* language Becky speaks. These are warning signs to activate your Weapons for Winning.

Remember that no matter how far along in the journey Becky is, she is still armed and dangerous.

Don't let Becky's fragility fool you; this White Fragility is a weapon, too. It serves one purpose: to manipulate you into feeling sorry for Becky. When you do she will abuse your grace by launching other weapons to harm you.

Don't Waste Your Magic: What do you know about Becky that you didn't know before?

_____

_____

_____

_____

_____

_____

_____

_____

_____

_____

_____

_____

_____

_____

_____

_____

"We may encounter many defeats **but** we must not be **defeated."**

-Maya Angelou

CHAPTER SEVEN

Emerging **from**

the Sunken Place

"Never **trust** anyone who says they do not see color. This means to them you are invisible." – Nayyirah Waheed

---

You can't win and exuberate with joy if you allow yourself to fall into the *Sunken Place*. The Sunken Place will snatch the precious breath from your body and leave you paralyzed in a painful state of stagnation, oppression, and depression. I know you've been in this place many times in your life. I've been there so many times I could spend the rest of my life counting and still not finish. Becky, Beckery, Beckyism, and the Weapons of Whiteness that white women use to deny, defend, and derail their racism can destroy you from the inside out.

Racism is emotional abuse. And like any other form of abuse, the effects are detrimental to your psychological, emotional, spiritual, and physical health. In my past career, I worked at two domestic violence and sexual assault programs. Both jobs gave me significant insights into the complex trauma experienced by domestic violence and sexual assault survivors. White Woman Violence produces the same kind of harmful effects as intimate partner abuse. The abusive tactics used by abusers and white women are the same, and the motive behind the abusive behavior is to create and maintain power and control over the victim.

Abusers use denial, blame, dominance, threats, intimidation, gaslighting, manipulation, and verbal assault to violate, harm, dehumanize, and oppress their victims. Doesn't this sound like the weapons white women use against women of color? Becky will deny her racism, blame you for your pain, violate you with dominance, manipulation, threats, and intimidation, and then try to manipulate you into feeling sorry for *her* by crying White Tears. And this is what you deal with when you engage with just *one* white woman. This frequent trauma leads you to experiencing Racial Battle Fatigue, and unaddressed emotional fatigue will sink you into the Sunken Place.

The Sunken Place is a soul slayer. It's a dark place that steals your dreams, smothers your joy, and forces you into a state of stagnation, oppression, and depression. Sister-friend, you can't be magical when you are in the Sunken Place! I firmly believe that we are all here to carry out a purpose and to fulfill our own unique destiny, but wallowing in and operating from the Sunken Place makes it impossible for us to carry out our special missions in life. When I refer to purpose, destiny, and mission I don't necessarily mean a big and extravagant act or event. Your existence is purpose enough. You are significant and don't have time to waste in the Sunken Place.

Writer and director Jordan Peele perfectly depicts White Woman Violence in his 2017 horror movie *Get Out*. Chris, a black man, is dating Rose, a white woman. Chris is diabolically lured to Rose's parents' house way out in the country to be hypnotized, lobotomized, and sold to rich white folks during the annual "buy a black person" auction. Yeah, ain't that some shit! While at the parents' house, Chris is repeatedly violated with insidious and intentional microaggressions by every white person there. At one point in the movie, Rose's mother, Missy, rhythmically stirs her tea cup to hypnotize Chris and demand that he sink into the floor! Upon her devilish command, Chris sinks through his chair, through the floor, and falls into a dark and bottomless space. He has full knowledge of what's happening to him, but in his hypnotized state, is unable to fight it.

Chris is violated, oppressed, and paralyzed in the Sunken Place. The sinister stirring of the tea cup transports Chris into a deep hole of terrifying despair. He knows what's happening to him, but he can't speak, scream, or cry out for help. He can't stop the sinking from happening, no matter how hard he desperately tries to liberate himself. Chris is in the Sunken Place for only a brief time; once he emerges, he senses he is in danger and needs to get out! But Chris fails to listen to his gut even with all the microaggressions going on and the uneasiness he feels. Eventually it becomes crystal clear that Rose purposely chose Chris to fulfill a blind white man's sick desire to have Chris' eyes so he can see again. Chris knows that if he doesn't get, out he will die or forever be doomed in the Sunken Place.

If you don't outsmart Becky when she draws her weapons on you, she will stir her treacherous tea cup of White Woman Violence and demand you sink into the Sunken Place! White Fragility, White Tears, and White Denial are Becky's favorite weapons, and she will use them to suck you into a deep, terrifying trance of madness and despair. She will first piss you off, then paralyze you, and finally blame you for being in the Sunken Place. Missy is a Becky too, and she has perfected the skill of inconspicuously stirring black folks into the Sunken Place. Missy, a good, well-intentioned white woman (or so she thinks), masterfully subdues her black victims with a smile on her face, just like all the other Beckys in the world.

There's something essential for you to know about Missy and the Sunken Place. In the movie *Get Out,* Missy does not stir black folks into the pit of hell in an overtly violent way. Nah, she uses a slick, sneaky technique with her refined and delicate teacup to suck the life out of you. Sometimes I think this type of Beckery is the most violent. Missy's violence is cunning, deceptive, and manipulative. In fact, doesn't Missy remind you of those Beckys you work with? Coworker Becky is one of the worst dream killers ever! White Woman Violence is an evil epidemic in the workplace. Coworker Becky will smile in your face and then use White Fragility to get you written up and fired. Coworker Becky will steal your ideas and claim them as her own. Coworker Becky will mistake your confidence as arrogance and aggression while whispering exaggerations in the boss's ear. Coworker Becky will pretend that she loves you, but will be threatened by your success and sabotage your every move. Coworker Becky will praise you to your face and assassinate your character behind your back. Coworker Becky will invite you to lunch and eat you alive in the dark. This is Becky. This Coworker Becky is Missy, and she is stirring the tea cup of violence to sink you into the Sunken Place.

When Becky in the workplace stirs her cup of violence and discharges her Weapons of Whiteness on you, you become uninspired, vigilant, and exhausted trying to get ahead at work. As a woman of color, you already have to work twice as hard and be twice as good as Becky. And when she passively or aggressively works to destroy you, you eventually find yourself in the Sunken Place. Yes, Sister, I know what this vicious cycle feels like. I've never had a job where Becky wasn't up to her tragic tricks. I left my last place of employment in 2008 at a predominantly white woman organization because of Beckyism. Those damn Beckys stirred me into the Sunken Place so many times that my lips would break out with cold sores, and I had a serious case of intermittent Irritable Bowel Syndrome.

I dreaded going to work every day, and I dreaded pretending that I enjoyed being there. I hated the sly, superficial small talk the white women engaged in. Coworker Beckys couldn't stand my audacity to defy them, and my strength scared them. Many of them would smile in my face, gossip behind my back, and pretend they cared, all while secretly wishing I would shut up and not call them out on their racist behavior. There was no chance in hell I would ever grant them that wish! I called them out unapologetically until my very last day. I knew it didn't make sense for me to go find another torture chamber (aka "job") to die in, and so I didn't. I took a blind leap of faith and started my own coaching and consulting business.

It's been a bittersweet journey being an entrepreneur for the last decade, yet I can't fathom having to make a living while dealing with Beckyism every day for the rest of my life. But I know that entrepreneurship is not for everyone. I'm not knocking your hustle, and I know you may have to work that job to provide for you and your family. You've got to do what you've got to do, and defying Becky and prioritizing your joy is critical to your ability to thrive! You may be considering leaving your job because of the Beckery, but know this: Beckys are everywhere! You can't run from them, because they will be at the next job, too. Entrepreneurship is about the only way to escape their wrath, and even then, you'll still have to deal with Becky at some point.

Have you ever been in the Sunken Place at work? You may be in the Sunken Place if you dread going to work and dealing with Beckys and *Brads* (white dudes). You may be in the Sunken Place if you're experiencing physical ailments due to work-related stress. You may be in the Sunken Place if you prefer eating your lunch in your office to avoid the Beckery. You may be in the Sunken Place if you have to minimize or subdue your culture to fit in. You may be in the Sunken Place if you've been "talked to" about being too difficult or aggressive at work.

One of the most powerful tactics used by white women to sink women of color into the Sunken Place at work and everywhere else is silence. In fact, White Woman Silence is one of the top five most used Weapons of Whiteness, and collectively white women have been using this weapon on women of color since forever. Not too long ago, I facilitated a SHETalks WETalk Race Talks for Women Workshop where most of the participants were white. During this two-day weekend workshop, every single one of the black women in the room shared their experiences of pain, struggle, horror, and oppression due to racism. These real-life stories caused tears of humiliation, desperation, and deep despair to surface in their expressions. As each brave woman shared her experiences, I looked around the room to see how the white women were reacting.

There were a few white women with tears welling up in their eyes. Yet most of them listened to the gut-wrenching stories of racial violence and emotional terror with blank, stoic stares. The white women in the room listened to the black women's pain without expressing any empathy or remorse. They sat silent. I don't recall even one of them saying "I'm sorry that happened to you," or any variation of it. However, when I called them out on their racism and use of weapons, they teared up and cried. White women could not FEEL the pain of these black human beings. Their violent silence sunk these black women into the Sunken Place. When I pointed out the violence in their silence, the white women were speechless. Those who did speak up admitted that they couldn't *relate* to the black women's pain.

How does one hear such raw pain and be emotionless? White women are disconnected from their humanity, and lack real empathy for women of color, especially black women. Part of the reason why white women do not empathize with black women is because of the centuries-old stereotype of the strong black woman. White folks have long believed and perpetuated the lie that black people don't feel pain or that we have a high pain tolerance; therefore, our pain is dismissed and minimized. In retrospect, as I recall the faces and body language of the white women in this workshop, I think they were in disbelief about the black women's expressions of pain. This further confirms my conclusion that white women don't give a damn about black women or any women of color. Becky has never been our sister. I'm not sure if she ever can be.

Becky is reckless and ravenous when it comes to black, brown, Native, and Indigenous lives. Remember the quote I used to introduce Chapter 4? Rachael Edwards is spot-on when she says, "*White women's racism will cut you in the dark and then ask you why you're bleeding.*" Psychologically speaking, the ability to do such harm to another human being and be in denial about the affliction is diabolical. That is not an exaggeration. At a minimum, as it relates to engaging with women of color non-violently, white women lack a sense of moral responsibility and social consciousness about the realities of women who are non-white. They do not have to know about us or our struggles. It's not a requirement that they learn how to effectively engage with black, brown, Native, and Indigenous women. We are simply an option for them that they can choose or ignore. Historically, white women never wanted us; they were just happy to make use of our servitude and labor. And this still remains true today.

To be in relationship with white women is to be in an abusive relationship, one with a repetitive cycle of violence occurring in your life. I have yet to meet a *safe* white woman. Why do white women do this? Why are they empathetically bankrupt? Why are they emotionally stoic about our real-life experiences? Why are they so damn fragile, yet extremely violent toward black, brown, Native, and Indigenous women? What the hell is wrong with Becky! I have two distinct answers among others already mentioned in previous chapters. First, Becky is operating from a place of internalized sexism. Second, she truly believes at a deep level that she is better than you. Becky is basking in and taking full advantage of her white supremacy Privilege.

Living in a patriarchal and male-dominated society causes women to fight for equality, equity, and power. In the quest for dominion, women will turn on other women who are also seeking to gain power, and will use the same violent weapons on those other women that men are using on them. This is common and oppressive behavior demonstrated by all women. I like to call it *trickle-down oppression*. Audre Lorde describes this phenomenon perfectly with one of her infamous quotes: "The master's tools will never dismantle the master's house. They may allow us temporarily to beat him at his own game, but they will never bring about genuine change." Audre is right! (By the way if you haven't read Audre's work, please start now!) I'll be using this quote to further expand on Becky, and again in a later chapter as a valuable piece of insight for women of color.

So, what does Audre mean when she speaks of the master's tools? Here's my conclusion. Within the societal and hierarchical systems, patriarchy tends to reign supreme. More specifically, white heterosexual men sit at the top of the hierarchy, and they hold most of the social and financial power in the United States. Because they hold the power and are in control, they abuse their power to oppress anyone who is not a white heterosexual male. All women have suffered under the thumb of white male oppression, including white women. And in turn, white women have internalized this patriarchal oppression and use the master's (white men's) tools to marginalize and oppress women of color. Couple this with their deep belief that they are better than non-white women, and you get White Woman Violence that sinks you into the Sunken Place.

Simply put, white women have mastered how to ignore, silence, discount, and violate black, brown, Native, and Indigenous women, just like white men do to them. And these same white men have also placed Becky on an untouchable pedestal deeming her superior to non-white women. Becky has been told she is the most beautiful, desirable, and honorable woman in the world and she believes it. She internalizes what I call *fool's gold:* the belief that because she is white, she is better and more deserving than other women. White women then spend their lives in this fool's bubble of oblivion, where they disregard, shut out, and tune out the needs, wants, and struggles of black, brown, Native, and Indigenous women. Beckys desperately and relentlessly chase the fool's gold while oppressing women of color in their quest for power. White women are experts in emotionally abusing women of color.

Sister-friend…Becky is *always* stirring her tea cup of violence. And if you're not careful, she will sink you into the Sunken Place. Becky is *always* armed and dangerous, no matter how nice she may seem. Becky is *always* capable of using Weapons of Whiteness against you, no matter how racially conscious she may speak. Becky may say the right things to make you believe she is sincerely a friend, but what she DOES is the *real* indicator of her sincerity about building a trusting relationship with you. James Baldwin, American writer and social critic, illustrates my point with a quote I love. He says, "I can't believe what you say, because I see what you do."

Please pay close attention to what Becky does. Don't be deceived by her words or you'll find yourself in the Sunken Place. In Chapter 6, I introduced you to some of the predictable statements you can expect from antagonistic white women. Guess what? There are so many of those that I have new statements for this chapter. Use these to alert you that Becky is stirring her teacup of violence. When you hear these, this is your cue to pull out your Weapons for Winning, the Four D's for Defying the Beckery: Dare, Disobey, Discontinue, and Detox.

- "Racism is not the real issue. Capitalism is."
- "Using the term White Fragility is racist."
- "People of color can be racist, too."
- "I might be willing to listen to you if you weren't so angry."
- "I don't do identity politics."
- "Not all white people."
- "When you talk about racism, you're creating division."
- "I grew up poor. I know all about your oppression."
- "I get it. I really do."
- "People of color need to stop acting like victims."
- "I am not responsible for what my ancestors did."
- "You're attacking me. I feel attacked."
- "Shaming me is not going to change things."
- "Maybe if he/she followed the officer's instructions he/she wouldn't have been shot."
- "People of color are only oppressed as much as they believe they are."
- "If you work hard, you can escape oppression."
- "White women are not your enemy, men are."
- "I don't whether you're black, brown, or purple."
- "When you talk about racism, you're being negative."

- "Don't you think you talk about racism too much?"
- "All this talk about racism is turning people away."
- "How am I supposed to learn if you don't teach me?"
- "Calling people out on their racism is not helpful."

When white women make these statements, they are denying your racial experiences and attempting to silence your truth. When Becky speaks this way, she is beckoning you into her teacup of terror. Don't fall for the treachery of her tricks. Don't allow yourself to be sunken. If you keep in mind that Becky knows only how to DENY, DEFEND, DERAIL, and DESTROY, then you will understand the conscious or unconscious intent behind her words and behaviors. Beckys come in many disguises, yet they are always wolves in sheep's clothing. Becky is the polite lady next door, your yoga instructor, your favorite sales clerk, the cool coworker, your sister-in-law, and every other white woman you engage with. They all have a teacup of terror!

Words are not the only weapons Becky uses. Her arsenal of weapons includes the invasive eye contact known as the White Gaze and other forms of aggressive and audacious body language. White folks will pierce your spirit with a look and a stare that blatantly says, "What are you doing here, you don't belong here, and what is *wrong* with you?" The White Gaze will question your existence in certain spaces (and if you're black, in every space), and white eyes will follow you in the store and assume you are a shoplifter. The White Gaze causes white women to clutch their purses and lock their doors in the presence of black and brown men. The White Gaze starts young, as evidenced by little white kids staring at you like they've seen a ghost. When Becky White Gazes you, it is another tactic to sink you into the Sunken Place.

Becky's violence has no boundaries or restraint. How many times have you been on the receiving end of the following aggressive body language:

- Have you ever been in line at the store and have a white woman cut in front of you like you're not standing there?
- Have you ever been waiting to be seated at a restaurant, then some white folks came in, and the white woman hostess shows them to

their table first?

- Have you ever been shopping for clothes and have a white woman clerk see you but not ask how she can help you?
- Have you ever had a white woman reach over you and violate your space without an "excuse me"?
- Have you ever had a white woman behind you in the checkout line who became irritated with you for no reason?

All of these non-verbal assaults are the stirring of the tea cup. To Becky you are invisible, irrelevant, and unworthy of acknowledgement. She's trying to sink you into the Sunken Place.

The whole point of Becky's tea cup of terror is to diminish your value, dismiss your presence, piss you the hell off, and paralyze you! Again, you might be thinking to yourself, "Not all white women, Catrice." But yes, I mean ALL of them, no matter how far on the Journey to Allyship they are. Remember my story in an earlier chapter? Maureen is a Becky too! There has NEVER been a time in history, including now, when white women were collectively held accountable for their crimes against black and brown humanity. And there has never been a time in history, including now, when white women have been collectively called out to face their racism and disarm their Weapons of Whiteness. But the time has come. And we must not waiver in our calling out. We must not tolerate this violence any longer. We must be unapologetic in demanding that Becky stop the violence, and we must make it clear that she will have earned the consequences if she chooses not to stop.

Sister-friend… you are NOT here to be consumed and paralyzed by the poison of Beckyism. You cannot allow the Beckery to steal your joy or stifle your dreams. You are here to be great. You are here to fulfill your destiny. You are here to carry out your purpose. You are here to live fully and love deeply. Don't let Becky mutilate your magic! Sometimes no matter how much you defy the Beckery, Becky will suck you into the Sunken Place. Here's a simple acronym to remind you that you are magic and you are here to win, something short and powerful to avoid and emerge from the Sunken Place. It's imperative that you WIN because the world needs you!

Cracking the BECKY Code Clues

WIN

Wake Up: Do not casually or unconsciously engage with white women. Remember that they are armed and dangerous with weapons to DENY, DEFEND, DERAIL, and DESTROY.

Ignite Your Weapons for Winning: Be prepared for the Beckery. You can DARE to speak, DISOBEY the Expectations, DISCONTINUE the Dialogue, and DETOX and Delight.

Never Give Away Your Magic: You don't have to defend your humanity. You don't need permission to be you. Be fierce. Be unapologetic. Stand strong. Refuse to give away your joy. *Don't waste your magic!*

Don't Waste Your Magic: How will you avoid getting sunk into the Sunken Place?

"I have **learned** over the years that **when** one's mind is made up, this **diminishes** fear; knowing what must be done does **away** with fear."

-Rosa Parks

CHAPTER EIGHT

Winning **when** Becky **comes for you**

"I am **deliberate** and afraid of nothing."
– Audre Lorde

Engaging with Becky is emotional and spiritual war. To win the war, you must be deliberate, unapologetic, and unafraid. Although history and current social dynamics indicate that going to war with white people can result in emotional, literal, and career death, do not let fear stop you from the equity, equality, freedom, justice, and liberation you desire and deserve. Always remember that it's not a matter of *if* Becky comes for you, it's *when* she comes for you; because she will, and with a vengeance. I know that dealing with the Beckery and anticipating dealing with Becky is exhausting as hell, but remember: you are here to WIN! To win you must be *deliberate* and afraid of NOTHING!

Let me help you understand what *Deliberate Fearlessness* looks like in action. As I discussed in Chapter 6, there is a universal violent language that white women speak no matter their geographic location. I call it the *White Woman Script*. I have yet to meet a white woman who does NOT use this self-centered and vile script when they engage with women of color, and I bet you've experienced this self-righteous script before, too. How is it possible for white women from everywhere to know and use this same script? The specific words they use to engage with women of color may be different, but the effect is always the same.

It's easy to identify the White Woman Script if you listen closely to the words that a white woman uses when she talks to you. Recently, I traveled to Portland, Seattle, Minneapolis, Chicago, and Milwaukee to host SHETalks WETalk Race Talks for Women Workshops. Although the white women in each workshop were different, the white violence was the same. In every single city, there were white women who cried White Tears, who stormed out and didn't return because of White Fragility, and who lashed out at me because of White Guilt and Shame. The white participants often sat with a deer-in-the-headlights look while exhibiting White Innocence. The workshop rooms were full of White Silence and White Centering. In other words, predictable and perfectly scripted White Woman Violence at every workshop.

White women have been given this sinister White Woman Script and they masterfully perform it. I'm talking about Academy Award-level enactments of martyrdom violence. Becky was the same no matter what city I was in, and she will be the same in every city I visit in the future. Believe me when I say that Becky will always be Becky no matter how much anti-racism work she claims to be doing. Do you remember the story I shared in Chapter 3 about Maureen, the white woman I was attempting to build a friendship with? Yeah, she's a Becky! I recently encountered another Becky who tried to camouflage her loaded weapons with perfectionism and politeness.

One of my white woman co-hosts for my workshops was eager to host, and extremely accommodating for six months. That all ended about a week after the workshop in her city took place. During the planning and implementation stages, she was friendly, helpful, responsive, and essentially non-violent. Usually I meet my co-host the first time I arrive in their city to host the workshop. Well, I first met Stacey at another workshop in a different city prior to the one being hosted in her city. During that first workshop she was mostly quiet, reserved, and a bit stoic. Her range of emotions was static. I wasn't exactly sure how to interpret her body language, but got the sense that she was emotionally constipated and that her body language and expression did not match her words. I chalked it up to her feeling uncomfortable with the content.

Upon engaging with Stacey in her home city, I noticed that her behaviors and responses were similar. Again I chalked it up to her feeling nervous and uncomfortable with my unapologetic blackness, and with my convictions about racism and White Woman Violence. Now, this was the workshop I described in the previous chapter, the one where black women in the workshop were sharing gut-wrenching stories of racial violence and oppression; the one where white women sat silent and expressionless, even though they cried like babies when they were called out on their White Woman Violence.

This part of the workshop was being filmed, and Stacey was caught on camera showing no emotion at all, just like the other white women in the room. She was completely stoic and unmoved by the anguish being expressed by black women. The event was being streamed on Facebook Live and comments about the white women started rolling in; they were being called out on their lack of empathy for black women's pain. After returning home from the workshop, I commented on the video and asked other white women to describe what they saw. The comments ranged from "inhumane" to "stoically violent." Absolutely nothing positive was stated about the white women's behavior in the workshop.

Stacey eventually chimed in; she owned her violence and claimed that she was going to do better at connecting to her humanity and her empathy for women of color. That was the last response I received from Stacey until a few days later. Stacey had been a part of my year-long program called the Journey to Allyship for several months. A few days after being exposed on video, Stacey posted a message in the program's Facebook group. She thanked me for all the anti-racism education she had received from me, and then stated that she was ending the program and seeking out other "resources" to learn. She exited the group and deleted me as a Facebook friend. I haven't spoken with Stacey since that message was written, and I do not plan to in the future.

Stacey could not handle the critique and callout of her inhumane behavior. Instead of owning it, being accountable for her actions, and working to find her humanity, she bailed. In typical Becky fashion, she got mad, took her toys, and left the playground. Stacey is Becky and Becky is Stacey. She followed the script of white fragility perfectly, and honestly, I was not surprised. Prior to her departure from the group, Stacey had written glowing testimonies about her workshop experience, had agreed to host another workshop in her city the following year, and was already promoting for the upcoming workshop.

It's clear to me that had I not called out her stoic, robotic behavior and her violence, Stacey would still be in the group and showing up as a performative "ally." A *performative* ally is a white person who shows up doing and saying all the *right* things to make people of color believe that they are doing *the work* (anti-racism work) and that they are on your side. They have digested just enough anti-racism ideologies and activist language to talk the language of deceit. It's deceitful because they are NOT doing the most important work, which is to uproot their own personal racism. Instead, they are performing external acts to create an illusion of evolution. These types of Beckys are extremely dangerous, and they are lethal! Their performative acts of concern, generosity, and support will stir you into the Sunken Place if you're not careful. Performative Beckys have no real interest in your pain or in doing their work. They just want to maintain their good white person personas so they can feel good about themselves.

I'm telling you, engaging with Becky on any level is to say *yes* to engaging in mental, emotional, and spiritual war. Seriously, you cannot let your guard down with these damn Beckys! They will take every morsel of kindness and grace you give them, and then destroy those gifts when they become challenged on their racism. Their default mode is always White Fragility and White Centering. Sister, I know you're tired, but you've got to win this war! One of the most effective ways to win the war against Beckery is to unlearn all the ways in which you've been indoctrinated into the *Serving Becky Syndrome*.

White supremacy has always positioned white women as superior, with women of color subservient to them, and white women have taken full advantage of their position. For centuries black, brown, Native, and Indigenous women were expected to put white women's needs, wants, and desires before their own or be subjugated to life-threatening consequences. White women abused their power and used it to oppress women of color. Black women in particular were forced to clean white women's houses, care for their children, and literally take care of white women before they cared for themselves, their children, their families, and their own homes. Black women were expected to obey Becky, be of service to her every whim, and to place *her* needs before their own.

Just as white women have been indoctrinated into believing and behaving as if they are better than black, brown, Native, and Indigenous people, we women of color have been indoctrinated into subconsciously believing that white is better. For centuries, if we wanted to get into and remain in certain spaces, especially workplaces, we have had to *shift* in the presence of white women. We've had to minimize our greatness, diminish our confidence, and make sure that Becky is not intimidated or offended. To learn more about this phenomenon, be sure to read *Shifting: The Double Lives of Black Women in America* by Charisse Jones and Kumea Shorter-Gooden. Women of color are required to shift as a matter of safety and survival in a white society.

When women of color shift, it is a form of *serving* Becky and putting yourself second. Shifting insists that women of color carefully choose their words and censor their language to be perceived as tolerable, less intimidating, and "professional." Shifting requires that women of color leave much of their culture at home so they can assimilate into white-dominated spaces. Shifting causes women of color to downplay their strengths so they don't appear too confident and assured, because those attributes intimidate white women.

Shifting demands that women of color silence, or at least diminish, their cultural language or ethnic attributes to appear more white, and thus more appealing, at work and within professional settings. Shifting causes women of color to abandon their true selves in order to cater to, *serve,* and please white folks. Shifting is exhausting; it is self-abuse in order to survive. One of the most detrimental aspects of shifting is that it forces you to deny your beauty, greatness, and brilliance to keep Becky and other white folks comfortable. When you shift, you actively engage in the Serving Becky Syndrome.

Audre Lorde ends her poem "Litany for Survival" with words that I think make the perfect statement about shifting and silence:

and when we speak we are afraid
our words will not be heard
nor welcomed
but when we are silent
we are still afraid
So it is better to speak

remembering
we were never meant to survive.
-Audre Lorde

Screw that! You don't have to shrink, shift, or be silent any longer. Shifting has allowed you to survive in a white society, but it has not necessarily kept you safe. Please stop settling for survival. You deserve to thrive, and to thrive you must unlearn these self-defeating survival skills and instead adopt effective tools to shut down the Beckery. You must be unapologetically you, and you must win!

I don't know about you, but I agree with Audre Lorde's lines above about the value of speaking even when we're afraid. As non-white women, we face a tremendous amount of legitimate fear as we navigate the world in our black and brown bodies. We know that just attempting this navigation is dangerous, let alone speaking up to defy racism and white supremacy. I truly understand the real danger and fear you experience. I also believe that if we're going to be afraid, it should be because we choose to speak up versus staying silent.

How to Unlearn Self-Defeating Survival Skills

Let me emphasize, I know how important the survival skill of shifting has been in your life. I have shifted countless times in my life; on occasion, I still do it, and I may do it in the future if I believe my safety is at risk. I don't deny the potency of this skill as a means of survival. Yet as I continue to refine and amplify my activist voice, I realize the importance of activating alternatives for moving beyond survival to truly thriving, not only professionally, but also personally. There may be times when the best thing you can do is survive, yet I want to offer you some tips on how to thrive in the face of White Woman Violence, especially Miss Anne's violence. In order to defy the Beckery you'll have to *unlearn* a few things.

- **Be Unsurprised.** By now you should have a clearer picture of who Becky is, how she operates, and why she does what she does. Refuse to be surprised and startled by her violent behavior. Remember that Becky is always armed and dangerous. She is never without her riot gear and her Weapons of Whiteness. **Stop being shocked by her violence!**

- **Be Unmoved.** Don't forget that Becky's weapons are used to DENY, DEFEND, DERAIL, and DESTROY, whether she draws them intentionally or unintentionally. Stand firm in your emotional grounding by knowing what her tactics are, and stay focused on counteracting them. Remember that you have the Weapons for Winning: Dare to Speak, Disobey the Expectations, Discontinue the Dialogue, and Detox and Delight. Don't let Becky discombobulate you! Whip out those Four D's for Defying the Beckery and be unmoved! **Stop letting Becky rattle you!**

- **Be Unbothered.** Becky and her Beckery is emotionally E.X.H.A.U.S.T.I.N.G! You must not forget that when Becky is using her Weapons of Whiteness, she is trying to stir you into the Sunken Place. To keep from sinking, you must be unbothered by her sinister shenanigans. Don't give away your emotional power. Stay buoyant! Refuse to sink. Instead of allowing yourself to be sucked into her vortex of violence, directly address and call out her offenses, and demand your respect. **Stop giving Becky your power!**

- **Be Unwavering.** To be unwavering means to be steadfast, firm, relentless, and unyielding. Being unwavering requires you to plant your feet on a solid foundation of clarity, confidence, and courage about who you are and the value you bring to the world. Being unwavering means to make it clear that if white people DO NOT respect your existence, there will be resistance. In other words, do not let Becky shake your foundation. Don't let her catch you slipping. Refuse to be sunken. Always, my Sister, always be firm and unwavering in your right to exist and to be unapologetically you! **Stop letting Becky break your stride!**

- **Be Unapologetic.** YOU ARE MAGICAL! You are beautiful, strong, resilient, brilliant, and valuable. No matter what others say about you, it is your right to exist safely and peacefully on this planet. White people do not get to define who you are. They do not get to determine your value. You do not need permission or approval from Becky on how you choose to show up in the world. You do not have to shift. You do not have to minimize or downplay your existence or magnificence. When you shift, minimize or subdue your presence, you are in effect apologizing for who you are. You do NOT have to do that any longer. Be unapologetic about your magic. Be unapologetic in every way possible, and do not be afraid to deliberately take up space, be seen, and speak your voice. **Stop diluting your magic!**

- **Be Unshakable.** Winning requires you to be unshakable! To be unshakable means to be UNSINKABLE. Do you hear what I'm saying to you? When you are unshakable, Becky cannot stir you and sink you into the Sunken Place. This is your *superpower* to resist her relentless wrath that aims to steal your joy and paralyze your power. I need you to be resolute in your right to exist without violence. I need you to be uncompromising about your greatness. I need you to do this not only for yourself, but also for all the black and brown women and girls watching you navigate in this world. Just as white women learn the White Woman Script from their mothers, aunts, sisters, and grandmothers, it is our duty as black, brown, Native, and Indigenous women to pass the MAGIC to our daughters, nieces, sisters, and friends. We stand on the shoulders of the resilient women who came before us, and one day we will be the shoulders upon which our daughters and granddaughters stand. Plant your feet, Sister. Be unbending, unrelenting, and unflinching in who and what you are! **Stop letting Becky break your foundation!**

- **Be Undeniable.** No matter how hard Becky tries, she cannot stop greatness; unless, of course, the great ones become paralyzed and sink into the Sunken Place. No matter how hard Becky tries to mask your magnificence, she can't unless you let her. Society has sold white women a fleeting fantasy called *fool's gold*. White society has made Becky believe she is the epitome of beauty, class, grace, and worthiness, and that all other women are second to her perceived greatness. Listen. Deep down inside, Becky knows the potency of not only YOUR beauty, but also your power. Why else do so many white women rape and pillage our cultures? Other than this fool's gold, what in the heck does it mean to be white? What is white culture? There is nothing clearly identifiable or significant that they haven't stolen from people of color. This is why Beckys co-opt our languages and cultures. You are undeniable! And to win you must unleash and amplify all that is culturally and unequivocally you. **Stop dimming your light!**

Time wasted on Becky is time you could spend being joyful. It's time you'll never get back. It's time she does not deserve. How you deal with Becky is up to you. You can choose to let her make you feel miserable, or you can maximize your magic.

When I was discussing "Be Undeniable," above, I brought up the point about white women craving culture and appropriating the cultures of people of color. And I asked, "What is white culture?" A significant number of people forfeited their ethnicity and culture to assimilate into mainstream whiteness. To survive they gave up their ethnic identity to become "white." But we people of color know that in a white world that is trying to destroy us at every turn, we must hold onto our ethnicity and culture. It's what keeps us alive inside. It's who we are, and because we are various shades of black and brown, we cannot hide or deny who we are.

As I mentioned in Chapter 4, my training and education is in psychology. I share this only to say that I know what I'm talking about when I talk about the psychology of Becky. In addition to having a lot in common with the clinical definition of narcissism (discussed in that previous chapter), white women also rely on a psychological defense mechanism called *reaction formation*. This psychological process is anchored in *psychoanalytical theory*, a theory of personality development and organization. This theory guides *psychoanalysis*, the clinical treatment of *psychopathology* (mental illness). Reaction formation is directly connected to neurotic defense mechanisms, such as disassociation, intellectualization, repression, and displacement. During reaction formation, anxiety-producing emotions and impulses that one views as unacceptable and/or unpleasant create exaggerated versions of the opposite emotions and impulses in that person. What does this mean? Let's use Becky as an example.

Subconsciously, all Beckys believe they are superior to women of color. They KNOW that having thoughts of superiority is wrong (unacceptable and/or unpleasant); therefore, most of them (unless they are explicitly racist) will masterfully exaggerate the opposite tendency and act like they like or love women of color. Let me put it another way. Becky truly thinks she is better than women of color (white society has instilled these false beliefs within her), but she also knows that this is NOT true, that she is not better than women of color.

To counteract her feelings of shame around this lie, Becky will behave in a way that allows her to feel *good* about her deception. She will say she's a good white person. She will take on a colorblind mentality. She will befriend black and brown people, and she will treat them as "human beings." In other words, Becky will go out of her way to make a point that she is NOT superior while deeply believing that she is. When Becky draws her Weapons of Whiteness after saying she adores you, this is reaction formation in action.

Becky has deep disdain for all women of color, but particularly for black women. To mask her anti-blackness, Becky may begin to fetishize black women and black culture. Remember Rachel Dolezal from Chapter 2? On the surface, Wanna-Be-Black Becky appears to love blackness, but when backed into a racist corner, the truth about this kind of Becky will be revealed (repression). She will draw her weapons no matter how much she claims to love blackness! Additionally, Becky knows that she has sold her soul for whiteness, and that she has traded in her ethnicity and culture for fool's gold. She further knows that whiteness is essentially cultureless. To counteract the pain of forfeiting her own magic, she instead chooses to belittle or borrow yours, and justifies this violence (intellectualization). The stealing of black and brown cultures lets Becky pretend she has roots. It makes her feel alive inside, because without cultural appropriation, who the hell is she (detachment)? The word *counterfeit* comes to my mind.

Listen, Sisters… once you decode Becky, you'll discover she is not as superior as she thinks she is. Don't believe for one second that Becky is superior. Becky is ignorant; in fact, she is often **willfully** ignorant. When she shows up with Weapons of Whiteness, know that she is operating from a place of disconnection from humanity, from being starved of culture, and from the fallacy of fool's gold. If you want to win, you must instantly and consistently move away from reacting emotionally to Becky's Beckery. Instead, be grounded in your magic, armed with logic and YOUR weapons, and channel your natural resiliency.

I've said it many times in this book and I'll say it again: engaging with Becky is exhausting. But you must win. You WILL win! Your equity, equality, freedom, justice, and liberation are tied up in your capacity, ability, and willingness to use your Deliberate Fearlessness. You know Becky's script. You see her riot gear. You know what her weapons are. You have insight into her psyche. You know Becky. And now, because you have Weapons for Winning and you've unlearned some old lessons, you can defy her with new effectiveness. So please, Sisters. Go forth with Deliberate Fearlessness and win!

Cracking the BECKY Code Clues

"Nah, Not Today Becky!"

Understanding what the Weapons of Whiteness are and how white women use them is an essential part of winning when Becky comes for you. Remember that to defy Becky, you must know her and the weapons she uses.

Sister, you're not here to SERVE Becky! Stop shifting around her. No matter where you are, and especially if Becky is present, firmly plant your feet, harness your power, own your presence, and demand respect. Becky ain't got nothing on you!

If you truly want to WIN, you've got to unlearn all of the ways that you've served Becky and allowed her to win. The choice is yours. Are you going to let Becky make you feel miserable or will you maximize your magic?

Don't Waste Your Magic: What is your plan to WIN?

_____

_____

_____

_____

_____

_____

_____

_____

_____

_____

_____

_____

_____

_____

"Is **solace** anywhere
more comforting
than that in
the arms of a **sister?"**
-Alice Walker

CHAPTER NINE

Stand **with** Your **Sisters**

"The master's tools will **never** dismantle the master's house."
– Audre Lorde

The first time I heard Audre Lorde's quote, "The master's tools will never dismantle the master's house," I was intrigued and puzzled. I wasn't exactly sure what she meant. In further examination of not only the quote, but the context in which she stated it, I unlocked a piece of the mystery of why women hurt and betray other women. As I discussed in Chapter 7 when I was talking about trickle-down oppression, my interpretation of her words is this. The master (white men) have become the masters of society by using tools (weapons) such as power, control, oppression, abuse, and marginalization to dominate white women and people of color. These tools not only helped white men take power and control, but their continued use allows them to keep it.

For centuries, white women have willfully and vicariously learned how to weaponize these tools, and just like white men, they still use them. Becky learned how to use these tools while they were being used against her. The very abuse white women receive from white men is the same abuse they inflict not ONLY on each other, but also on black and brown women and men. The abuse doesn't stop there. Black, brown, Native, and Indigenous people internalize this abuse and then use these same violent tools against each other, which results in internalized oppression and interracial violence. Yes, this is one treacherous cycle of violence we're in, folks. We are using the master's tools against each other.

And while we continue to harm and oppress one another, white men are sitting back and watching the violence they've brilliantly orchestrated, violence from which they reap so many benefits. While we fight among ourselves, they are creating policies and enacting laws that will continue to oppress and marginalize us. And while we fight over who is more oppressed, white women continue to uplift white supremacy and stay protected under the cloak of whiteness. White women will **never** be able to create unity and solidarity with black, brown, Native, and Indigenous women because they are using the master's tools against us. And we will never be able to create unity and solidarity among ourselves as women of color, because we are using the master's tools against each other. THIS must stop! We must stop the cycle of violence against one another or none of us will truly WIN.

"The master's tools will never dismantle the master's house. They may allow us temporarily to beat him at his own game, but they will never bring about genuine change." – Audre Lorde

---

Black, brown, Native, and Indigenous women continue to bicker with and fight one another. Meanwhile, because of our ignorance, white women continue to maintain power and privilege at our expense. Yes, ignorance. I don't mean *ignorance* in the sense that you're stupid. I mean *ignorance* in the sense that you may lack knowledge and information, and this lack keeps you an active perpetrator in the cycle of violence. I was once quite ignorant about how I too used the master's tools violently against my own black people. I can recall two very specific ways in which I weaponized my "light-skinned privilege," and I'll tell you more about them a little later in this chapter Yes, in the past I used colorism to discriminate against other black people, including family members.

Colorism, a term coined by Alice Walker in 1982, is prejudice and discrimination based on skin tone and primarily occurs in communities of color. Scientifically speaking, race isn't a real thing. There is only one race, the human race. Underneath the myth of racism is the real issue of skin color. People don't face prejudice because they have a governmental designation of a particular race, but they do face prejudice because of the actual color of their skin. As the browning of America continues, race as a social construct will become even more irrelevant. However, prejudice and discrimination based on skin color is likely to prevail. Because of white supremacy and the false idolization of whiteness, the closer your skin color is to white, the more privilege and power you hold, whether you want it or not.

That's messed up! We people of color have bought into this vicious and oppressive lie. White and light-skinned people are NO better than people with darker skin. This is a violent untruth and we MUST stop believing and perpetuating it. I used to perpetrate this lie and the violence to go with it. My only biological brother has darker skin than I do. His skin tone is about the same as the gorgeous Idris Elba (swoon). I vividly remember when my brother and I would argue about whatever, and my first clap back or put-down to him would be some derogatory comment about his dark skin, his blackness. It would enrage him, and I remember my words would paralyze him momentarily, until he'd fire back at me with fat-shaming comments.

We used these horrible weapons against each other for years. When I wanted to hurt him, I attacked his blackness. When he wanted to hurt me, he attacked my fatness. When I think about my use of prejudiced weaponry against my own brother, it's saddening. I've since made amends for this abuse, and this experience forms part of my own Awakened Conscious Shift. I know I deeply wounded him and compounded the racist societal attacks he experienced growing up. At such a young age, I was ignorant about how the world really perceived his blackness and how he was treated outside of our home because of it. I didn't know the impact of my behavior and had no idea I was adding fuel to his painful fire.

I didn't know I was using the master's tools against my own flesh and blood, but I was. Where did I learn this violence? My mother NEVER taught me I was better than my brother because I had lighter skin. How did this transfer of violence enter my psyche? I wasn't taught this abuse, yet I had mastered it. Whether you want to admit it or not, the same violence has been transferred into your psyche, too. You've become a master at colorism, just like me. We've been infected with the virus of white supremacy in our own unfortunate way. We must rid ourselves of this virus, because it's killing us and suffocating our collective strength to thrive and win. White supremacy is counting on us to keep fighting each other so that we stay oppressed.

Just as white women are indoctrinated into white supremacy with their first out-of-the womb breath, we are indoctrinated into colorism with our first breath. We learn immediately that "white is right" and everything else is *other* and inferior. We learn how to celebrate versions and variations of whiteness, and we vilify blackness and darkness. We vicariously learn from society, parents, teachers, friends, and others the mythical value and unearned appreciation given to whiteness and lightness. We find our place on the spectrum of skin tone and begin to act accordingly. We have willfully picked up the master's tools and perpetrated violence against those darker than us, while secretly hating or fetishizing those lighter than us. WE have done this. YOU have done this.

Colorism is not unique to the United States. Colorism is widely and pervasively used as a weapon in Africa, India, Asia, the Caribbean, Latin America, and every place in between. We've learned how to use skin color as a dehumanizing criterion to determine one's value and treatment. You may have even used the weapon of colorism on yourself, which is a form of self-abuse. Where do you place yourself on the hierarchy of color? Have you judged your fellow melaninated sisters based on the color of their skin? Have you settled for less, or put up with violence, because your skin is dark? Have you allowed yourself to treat lighter-skinned sisters with disdain because their complexion is closer to whiteness? I'm sure that you have been, like I have been, both the victim and the perpetrator of colorism.

From the first time I began to take an intimate interest in boys, my preference was always for light-skinned black boys. I believed they were more attractive and worthy of my time. This was the second time I weaponized my light-skinned privilege, because I didn't give dark-skinned boys the time of day. And quite frankly, I wasn't too interested in dark-skinned girls as friends, either. I had absolutely no interest in dating or befriending anyone whose skin was darker than mine. My ignorance led me to believe I was better than them. I'm not sure exactly what spawned my colorism wakeup call, but I clearly remember it happening a year after I graduated from high school.

Something shifted internally for me shortly after I graduated from high school. Seriously, I cannot pinpoint anything in particular that woke me up from the discrimination and violence I was perpetrating against my own people. But thank God I began to wake up! My social awakening has significantly evolved since that time. I clearly see how colorism rears its hideous head specifically in relationships and engagements between black, brown, Native, and Indigenous women (people). Not only are you wasting your magic on Becky, you're stealing the magic of your sisters and oppressing them through colorism. There is a lot of truth that needs to be spoken about the potency of the pain this violence causes. THIS is our work to do for ourselves and our sisters.

"What woman here is so enamored of her own oppression that she cannot see her heel print upon another woman's face? What woman's terms of oppression have become precious and necessary to her as a ticket into the fold of the righteous, away from the cold winds of self-scrutiny?" – Audre Lorde

---

Becky and Brad have passed along these master's tools to generation after generation of people of color. You may have consciously and/or unconsciously picked them up and used them. Today I want you to identify these treacherous tools and LAY THEM DOWN. You spend so much time dealing with and trying to defy Becky that you forget that you, too, have become weaponized. And let me reiterate this truth: Becky and Brad want you to be in conflict with your black and brown sisters to distract you from the tricks, schemes, and sinister shenanigans they conjure up for your demise while you fight with each other. Don't fall for the game. If we're going to WIN, we must all win.

Audre Lorde asks us not to only be cognizant of our own oppression, but also to remember that our black and brown sisters are facing their own unique forms of oppression. She challenges us to see our heel print on another woman's face and to essentially check ourselves to determine if WE are part of her oppression. If we discover that we are, it is OUR work to remove our heel from her face, make amends, and work toward reconciliation and repair. What I've noticed as a significant barrier to fostering unity and solidarity between women of color is the active participation in *Oppression Olympics*.

Let me give you an example of what the Oppression Olympics looks like in real life. Let's say you share with me that you've been physically assaulted once by your partner, and my response to you is something like, "Well, you don't know real abuse, because I've been physically assaulted by *every* partner I've ever had." If I respond to you this way, I'm saying that your abuse is not as bad as mine because yours happened only once. It's a horribly violent game of *let's see who is the most oppressed* while discounting the pain and suffering of another marginalized person. This is not cool. It's dismissive and violent, and black and brown people are doing this to each other every day. We have our heels on the faces of other black, brown, Native, and Indigenous people and are playing a harmful game of Oppression Olympics.

Now let me make this point clear. It is important to know about and point out specific forms of oppression that each ethnic group faces. It's important to talk about the differences. It's essential to highlight the unique ways in which the various groups have been violated and marginalized. In America, two particular ethnic groups come to mind. There is absolutely no doubt that the genocide and damn near annihilation of the Native peoples of North America is a horrendous atrocity. This evil didn't just happen to them decades ago. They still face overwhelming challenges and barriers in every aspect of their lives.

Additionally, we cannot deny the centuries of barbaric chattel slavery endured by black people in this country. We should not minimize the rape, murder, beatings, and lynchings that black folks experienced for almost three hundred years, and we should not forget that they were bought and sold like cattle. Black folks are still suffering from the lingering effects of slavery. I could go on about every black and brown ethnic group in this country, but it would require me to write another book. My point with these two ethnic groups is that we people of color have had vile and vicious violence inflicted upon us. You can acknowledge and advocate for your people's pain while not putting your heel on the face of another woman of color.

You will NOT win with your foot on another woman's neck. You may achieve some temporary gain, but you will not WIN. And guess what? There is enough of everything for all of us to win. There is no shortage of attention, promotions, lovers, money, and recognition. We all can have it all when we help each other win. We can and should be our sister's keeper. Here's what I know to be true about the collective Becky. They don't want us to win. They don't want us to lay down the master's tools that we use against each other. The collective Becky and Brad have front row seats to one of the greatest social fights in the ring of life: black and brown people fighting among themselves.

While we fight, Becky and Brad maintain the power, privilege, and control. We people of color are being used as puppets and pawns against each other to keep the master's house intact. You *cannot* dismantle the master's house with the master's tools!

- Which tools of violence are you using against black, brown, Native, and Indigenous women?
- In what ways are you silencing their voices?
- How are you marginalizing them?
- How have you discounted, disregarded, and devalued their experiences?
- Have you allowed colorism to infect you?
- Have you internalized your oppression?

Silencing another woman of color's voice is a tool of the master. Pushing another woman of color's issues and struggles to the side is a tool to oppress her. Discounting the lived racial experiences of a woman of color is a tool of the master. Devaluing the oppression faced by a woman of color is a tool to commit violence against her. Treating a woman of color poorly because of the color of her skin is a tool of the master. And when you believe YOU are better than or less than because of the color of your skin, you are using the master's tools against yourself. All of these behaviors are forms of violence against women and yourself.

Tools You Might Be Using to Oppress Other Black and Brown Women

How many master's tools have you used against your sister?

_____Judging her value or worth based on skin tone.

_____Refusing to be genuinely happy for her.

_____Feeling threatened by her success.

_____Ridiculing the color of her skin, also known as **skin-shaming**.

_____Blaming her for her poverty or lack of education.

_____Criticizing her because of the number of kids she has.

_____Judging her value based on where and how she lives.

_____Believing you are better because you're lighter or darker.

_____Assuming that a lighter-skinned woman thinks she is superior.

_____Criticizing how she looks or dresses.

_____Making fun of the way she talks.

_____Tone policing her or correcting her grammar.

_____Questioning her level of commitment to her race.

_____Saying, "She's pretty for a _____ woman."

_____Criticizing the texture or length of her hair.

_____Making fun of her facial features.

_____Believing that your racial struggle is worse than hers.

_____Invalidating and/or minimizing the level of oppression she faces.

_____Excluding her because she's too dark or light.

_____Making fun of her dialect or accent.

_____Throwing "shade" at her or giving backhanded compliments.

_____Believing the stereotypes about her race or culture.

_____Making fun of her culture.

_____Buying into the Angry Black Woman trope.

_____Expecting her to act a certain way based on her race or culture.

_____Accusing her of acting white.

Whew! As I wrote this list, so many instances of violence came to mind, instances where I was the oppressor, and instances where I was the oppressed. I thought about ways that I've caused pain, and ways that I've been hurt by this ignorance and foolishness. I literally could have kept writing for days and the list would not be complete. We've been strategically programmed and encouraged by the master to think and behave in this nasty and hurtful way to one another. We must actively and consistently work to unlearn this violence and diligently lay down these tools of destruction. If you are engaging in this type of interracial violence, you are oppressing your sister and you will NOT win, no matter you justify this lethal behavior.

Being conscious of your prejudices against other women of color takes intentional effort. I work on laying down my tools every day, and it takes a lot of mental energy to evaluate my biases and choose another thought or action. I CAN do better, and so can you. I'm rooting for all of us, and I want all of us to win regardless of our race, ethnicity, and how we show up in the world. When we engage violently with each other, Becky and Brad will *always* win. Haven't they been winning enough? This type of malicious behavior doesn't dismantle the master's house; it strengthens the foundation and lifts it up. And the stronger the master's house gets and the higher it rises, the more people of color are marginalized and disenfranchised. If you want to be free, you must help your sister get free!

"I am not free while any woman is unfree, even when her shackles are very different from my own."
– Audre Lorde

Can you clearly see how the master is orchestrating this game of deadly distraction? We're all caught up in a callous game of social chess, and Becky is the queen. Don't get it twisted! I don't mean *queen* in the sense of royalty and prestige. Becky is the powerful piece in the game that supports the deceitful king's deadly plan to destroy us. White women since forever have been in cahoots with the king (the master) to keep women (people) of color oppressed and marginalized. If we don't stop fighting with each other,

THEY will continue to win. It's time to de-weaponize yourself and stand with your sisters: ALL of them. We have absolutely nothing to lose when we do, but *so* much to gain. And of all the things you can gain from standing with your sisters, JOY is one of the most important.

It's not enough to be content or happy. It's not enough to be satisfied. I want you to consistently experience pure, unadulterated, and profound joy every single day for the rest of your life. And I'm not talking about basic joy. I want you to experience bliss, exuberance, jubilation, elation, exhilaration, and delight. Yes, that kind of euphoric joy! Seriously, how can you experience all of this soul-lusciousness when you have your boot on another woman's face? You can't. Get your boot OFF her back! As a matter of fact, just take the boots off already! The war you need to be fighting is not between you and your sisters. Put down those tools! Don't help the master build his house. De-weaponize yourself, starting now. You are *here* to win, my Sister, and in order to win, you're going to need your sisters. Now is the time to amplify *her* and your joy!

Cracking the BECKY Code Clues

"Nah, Not Today Becky!"

One of the most powerful and lethal tools of the master is anti-blackness. If the United States were built upon two pillars, they would be white supremacy and anti-blackness. Those two treacherous threads created and maintain the fabric and foundation of this country. Anti-blackness is not limited to white people. Everyone has anti-blackness in them, including black people. White supremacy has infected us all with the deep-seated belief that black is bad and inferior.

Non-black women of color, you have anti-blackness within you. Who did you learn this from? How does your anti-blackness show up? What beliefs do you have about darker-skinned women? You must dig up these violent tools and never again use them against your darker-skinned sisters and yourself.

Black women, you have anti-blackness within you. Who did you learn this from? How does your anti-blackness show up? What beliefs do you have about dark-skinned black women? You must dig up these violent tools and never again use them against your black sisters and yourself.

Sisters, we are spending too much time on the battle field of Oppression Olympics and not enough time preparing ourselves for the Becky war. Own your anti-blackness, uproot it, and lay down your anti-black weapons. There can be no solidarity without unity. Stand with your sisters. We're on this journey to joy together!

Don't Waste Your Magic: How will you stand with your sisters?

_____

_____

_____

_____

_____

_____

_____

_____

_____

_____

"We will be ourselves and free, or die in the **attempt.** Harriet Tubman was not our great-grandmother for **nothing."**

-Alice Walker

CHAPTER TEN
Amplifying
Your **Joy**

"Don't wait around for other **people** to be happy for you. Any happiness you get you've go to make yourself." – Alice Walker

---

Since I started doing my social and racial justice work, it's become clear to me how much more ALIVE women of color are than white women. In Becky's relentless pursuit of fool's gold, she has not only sold her soul to the master, she has died inside. Maybe Becky was never alive to begin with. Seriously! When you think about all of the atrocities that have happened to black, brown, Native, and Indigenous women over the centuries, how could white women collectively stand by and do nothing? This leads me back to questions I have asked online, in my workshops, and in this book, and that I will continue to ask:

- Has there ever been an undeniable, clearly documented time in American history when white women have collectively put their lives on the line to speak up for, and advocate on behalf of, black and brown women?
- Have they ever collectively sacrificed their time, energy, money, and resources to stand in the gap for black and brown women?

The answer has always been no; it's still no.

The refusal of white women to show up as our so-called sisters in the fight is painfully telling. They've made their voices loud and callously clear: the collective Becky doesn't give a damn about black and brown women. There's no significant history or current action to make me believe otherwise. It is what it is. Becky cares only about herself. She doesn't even really care about other Beckys. Only women with apathetic souls could sit silently while black and brown women are stolen, bought, sold, raped, mutilated, beaten, lynched, demeaned, silenced, and dehumanized at every turn. To be the actual perpetrators of such horrendous acts means they lack humanity and the conscious capacity to empathize with human suffering. White women have not only been bystanders of the violence against black and brown women, but also the perpetrators.

On the other hand, what amazingly fantastical women YOU are! You have been forced into the eye of the storm of violence, yet you still love humanity! Yes, dear Sister, you may not always feel like loving or being loved, but the capacity to do so is there for you to access any time you choose. You may be angry, sad, or bitter, yet you are still deeply connected to your humanity. Unlike Becky, you are already connected to the source of JOY: the love of people regardless of what they look like. In my work with white women, I'm quick to remind Becky that they are NOT disconnected from their humanity, because they never had it. They need to find it for the first time and stop chasing fool's gold.

Sister… you are already winning! As rough as life may get and as hard as you have to fight to simply exist, you ARE ALIVE inside. Hell, you have been resisting and persisting ever since you took your first breath. You are winning because you are strong and resilient. Becky don't know nothing about REAL resistance and persistence. Maya Angelou reminds us of our tenacity and our capacity to *still rise* with her powerful quote, "You may encounter many defeats, but you must not be defeated." The only way you'll be defeated is when you choose to NOT WIN. And remember, winning is not about the attainment of material possessions, but instead is about being **you** unapologetically, maximizing your power, and refusing to relinquish your magic and joy!

Remember the story of Stacey at the workshop, the one where white women showed up void of empathy and humanity as black women poured out their pain? Well, as maddening as that situation was, something else happened at the workshop, something that was beautifully human. On the second day of the workshop, I asked the white women to share reflections they had from the first day. Many of them shared insights they had gained, and a few women shared personal conversations they'd had with their children about racism. One woman said that she looked at her granddaughter with new eyes and thought to herself, "I better start working with her while she's still young so she can connect with her humanity." Another woman said that she shared the importance and urgency of laying down her weapons now with her adult daughter, before it's too late and she causes harm.

As these two white women shared the experiences they'd had with their families, I noticed a black woman covering her face and looking away from the white women with tears in her eyes. I'll call her Bella for *beautiful one*. When I asked her why she was tearful, she said she didn't want the white women to see her cry, because they had not cried for her and the other black women who had shared heart-breaking pain. I understood exactly what Bella meant and why she didn't want the white women to see her tears. I moved toward her and validated her truth. I challenged Bella to not allow their refusal to acknowledge black pain to make her inhumane like them. I reminded her that the ability to feel another's pain and to show empathy is beautifully human. I affirmed Bella's beautiful human-ness and encouraged her to keep being human.

"Bitterness is the coward's revenge on the world for having been hurt." – Zora Neale Hurston

---

Becky can't see or feel your pain, and she's highly likely to not cry for you. You know what I say to that? So. The. Hell. What! You don't need her White Tears to validate your humanity. Maybe you've felt like Bella before. I have and sometimes still do, but I refuse to allow the Beckys of the world to make me bitter. Sister-friend, do NOT be bitter. Continue to be *beautifully human*, always. Have you ever been mad at someone, but they continue to be happy in spite of your anger? Man… doesn't that frustrate the hell out of you? Well listen, that's what you have to do with Becky. You must be happy and express joy in spite of her Beckery! Don't waste your magic! This is how you WIN.

On my journey of speaking out about racial justice, people have walked away from me, disconnected from me, tried to silence my voice, and attacked me. Some have had the damn audacity to try to smother my voice with the Angry Black Woman cloak. Nope. I refuse to live up to this stereotype, even when I'm angry as hell about the injustices black and brown people face every single day. What most people don't know is that doing **this** work and using my gifts and voice *this way* brings me immeasurable joy! I am created and called to do *this work*. Racial justice work unleashes the pure, unadulterated, and profound joy within me, even when Becky tries to stir me into the Sunken Place. Even though Becky stirs her cup of terror all around me, I am still winning!

Are you going to let Becky keep you from all of the bliss, exuberance, elation, and delight that you can stand? Nah! Not today, Becky! When you hear the clang of her tea cup attempting to stir you into the Sunken Place, that's what you need to say: "Nah! Not today, Becky!" As a matter of fact, this can be your motto in every single moment when engaging with Becky. Your emotional energy is precious. It's your life source. Use it wisely, and don't waste your magic on Becky. Before reading this book, you already knew what was happening to you. You knew that Becky and her Beckery was a toxic force in your life. You knew she was smiling in your face and stabbing you in the back. You're not delusional. All of this violence is happening to you, but now you have words to speak about it and weapons to defy it.

One of my favorite sayings of Iyanla Vanzant's is, "Call a thing a thing!" That means tell the truth. Give the truth a name and call it out in order to clearly identify what it is. Beckery and Beckyism is that thing in your life that's stealing a big piece of your joy. Almost everywhere you go, you will deal with Becky on some level, and it's extremely likely she will White Gaze the hell out of you, cut in front of you in line, totally ignore your presence, draw weapons on you, and/or attempt to stir you into the Sunken Place. By now I hope you are clear about the toxicity of engaging with Becky. And I hope that when Beckery occurs, you will call a thing a thing and use your Weapons for Winning to defy her Beckyism and decrease your Racial Battle Fatigue.

Listen, Sister. I know some days you give all you can just to survive. I know that it may seem like you're never getting ahead in life. You may be overwhelmed with the daily requirements to just get through the day. I know it feels like it's you against the world sometimes. I know how you feel when racism just won't seem to stop throwing punches at you. There so many more important things to give your energy to and to worry about. I get it. I really do. I feel your pain and struggle, because sometimes your pain and struggle is my pain and struggle. Your story is different and your life circumstances are unique. Yet when it comes to surviving the Beckery, I have walked in your shoes.

Let's go back to this beautifully human reality. Although Becky gets on my last nerve all the damn time, I believe destiny is a choice in spite of your circumstances. What do I mean by that? I mean there is no way in hell I'm going to let Becky block my blessings, derail my destiny, or strangle my joy. No matter what weapons she draws on me, she WILL NOT WIN. I hope you choose to adopt this unwavering commitment to winning in your life. The joy you seek won't come from material possessions. Obtaining things may bring you happiness. But deep, profound, and throbbing joy comes from connections and relationships with people, not things. Do not let Becky make you bitter!

"In a world that directly and indirectly tells Women of Color they are not worthy, qualified, invited, beautiful, or valued, we must deny EVERY restriction, affliction, prediction, and depiction that causes us to stay captive, be unhealed, doubt our destiny, and fail to embrace our beauty." – Catrice M. Jackson

---

Don't let your circumstances make you bitter. You can choose peace no matter how much Beckery you have to deal with. You can choose joy no matter what your circumstances are. Remember that one of your Weapons for Winning is to Detox and Delight. If you're not sure how to choose peace and joy, I hope you find the following tips helpful in learning how to cultivate, sustain, and amplify your joy. Your capacity to experience joy begins and is sustained in your heart, not your mind. And if you let Becky harden your heart, you will NOT be able to experience the joy you desire.

Tips for Cultivating, Sustaining, and Amplifying Your Joy

Cultivate Your Soul: I imagine that years of frustration, sadness, and anger due to Beckyism have taken an emotional toll on you. Or maybe you believe you've done a good job at not allowing Becky to affect your emotional and mental well-being. But if thoughts and feelings of resentment, cynicism, unforgiveness, and anger easily emerge when you think of Becky, you have allowed the residue of her wrath to take root in your soul. Such roots are detrimental to the survival of your joy. You're sure to harvest bitterness from those roots, which will contaminate other relationships with people you love. Joy is in your heart; don't let it become hardened.

What happens when you don't cultivate your soul and dig up this Beckyism? You're at a greater chance of developing anxiety, depression, or post-traumatic stress disorder (PTSD). So listen, Sister, you've got to do this for YOU, not for Becky's sake. I need you to dig deep in your soul and release any anger and bitterness you have about Becky. Let that crap go! Harboring hate toward Becky will literally make you sick. She is NOT worth your health. You've been given the tools to WIN. Activate them!

Plant New Seeds: Joy has to have a place to grow and thrive. Your bitterness toward Becky will certainly prevent you from producing the sweet and exuberant joy I know you want to experience. Becky is not as powerful as she thinks she is, and she does not have power over you! Believe the Alice Walker quote that says, "Nobody is as powerful as we make them out to be." Are you really going to give your power away to someone who's chasing fool's gold? Take back your power today.

Remember, I said that in order to defy Becky, you need to know her. You need to know her intentions, the weapons she uses, and why she uses them. Now you know. You no longer have to be a victim of her venom. I need you to plant all of what you've learned deep in your soul so it can blossom, instead of allowing Beckyism to brood within. The next time Becky comes for you, plant your feet, harness your power, call a thing a thing, and discharge your

Weapons for Winning. Show up and engage with Deliberate Fearlessness! You've got this!

Get Plenty of Sunshine: It's going to take some confidence and courage to defy Becky this way, especially if she is your boss or coworker. You're going to need to master your own way of defying Beckery. You won't do it like I do, or like any other woman of color does, and you shouldn't. Be sure to surround yourself with other sisters in the fight so you can draw wisdom and strength from them. They need you and you need them. Yes, dealing with the Beckery is exhausting, but don't let it consume you. I know that's easier said than done sometimes, because Becky is maddening. Be sure to get plenty of sunshine! What makes you happy? What brings you peace? What are your favorite escapes? Who makes you smile? What are you passionate about? When Becky's racism cuts you in the dark, go to your sunshine.

Let's make this as simple as possible. When Becky comes for you, here's what you can do:
1. Identify the weapon(s) she is using.
2. Know and understand the intent behind the weapon and decide how you'll respond.
3. Activate your Weapons for Winning.
4. Detox and Delight (Weapon for Winning #4). In other words, follow the advice in this chapter.
5. Bask in the sunshine, my Sister! Also known as, *shake it off and sink into your joy spot!*

Water Daily: As you already know, following the five steps above won't put an end to the Beckery. You'll encounter Becky again and again. But the more you put this practice into motion, the easier it will become and the less stressed you will be. Before you know it, you'll be slaying Beckys left and right! Yes! You'll become a Ninja Becky Slayer!

Seriously, having to defy Becky every day is mental and emotional war. It's not called Racial Battle Fatigue for nothing. You don't have to fight every

Becky battle, and you shouldn't if you want to win in the long run. It's essential for you to water your spirit every day. It's critical that you nourish your soul by deepening the connections with your ethnic roots and culture. Oprah Winfrey says, "Turn your wounds into wisdom," and she's right. The women elders who came before you suffered many wounds for you to be here. There is great solace, comfort, inspiration, and wisdom in the teachings of the women who paved the way for you. Reconnect to that source daily. Link up with other black, brown, Native, and Indigenous women to give and receive support. Study your ethnic history more deeply and let the brilliance of your ancestors help you defy Becky. Trust me, they know the way!

Here are a few ways to water daily:

1. Know your history. Study your culture's, family's, and personal history. Study your country's history. Study world history. Why? Because when you know the truth about *who* you are, then no one, absolutely no one, can make you feel inferior. Knowing your history helps you anchor into your truth, value, and worth.

2. Rest and get enough sleep. Did you know that your body detoxes itself when you sleep? If you're not getting enough sleep, you're not replenishing your body. Life is stressful enough, and dealing with Becky increases your stress. Take breaks. Sneak in a nap. Take time away from social media. Rest, Sister, rest.

3. Access your creative outlets. What do you love to do? What are your natural gifts? Do you like to sing, dance, or paint? Spend more time doing whatever you love to do. If it's been forever since you've done it, get back to it! Creative outlets provide an escape from the stresses of life, connect you to your joy spot, and inspire your hopes and dreams. Take up a new hobby. Turn your frustrations into art. Use creative outlets to express yourself and to decompress.

4. RECLAIM YOUR TIME, by any means necessary! Limit the time and energy you give to Becky. Don't forget that you are not a social experiment. You are not a toy to be played with. You are not an emotional punching bag, and you are not a guinea pig for Becky's research. Reclaim your time and use it for the activities and people

who bring you joy!

5. Put yourself at the top of the list. What can you do to protect your magic and amplify your joy? How can you nourish yourself daily? Feed your body good food. Indulge in your favorite books. Incorporate more movement into your day. Meditate. Do whatever it takes to take care of YOU, always!

6. Unleash your magic! Yes Sister, you are magic! Here are few ideas to activate and amplify your magic from my book *Unleash Your Significance: Activate the Audacity to Be All You Are Destined to Be.*

Do you know *how powerful and special* YOUR magic is? *You are rare and can never be duplicated, ever!* That is pure magic all by itself. Can you imagine what your life will be like when you embrace this powerful truth? You are rare, pure magic! So, what is magic?

- Magic is turning your words into experiences.
- Magic is moving a dream from distant thought to an intimate reality.
- Magic is making the invisible tangible and touchable.
- Magic is predicting how your life turns out.
- Magic is transforming your physical body and restoring your vitality.
- Magic is purging your soul from everything that paralyzes your purpose.
- Magic is doing work you love and loving the work you do.
- Magic is leaping out of your comfort zone into the unknown and thriving.
- Magic is turning limiting beliefs into limitless possibilities.
- Magic is creating harmony within, and living your own unique melody.
- Magic is creating and experiencing moments that take your breath away.
- Magic is trusting that your soul knows the way and following it.
- Magic is saying, "So what?" and living your life unapologetically.
- Magic is slowing down and savoring the silence and synchronicity of life.
- Magic is hearing the whispers of the divine one and saying, "Yes!"

- Magic is unleashing your gifts and serving the world with them.
- Magic is *not giving a damn* what other people think of you.
- Magic is making a meaningful contribution to humanity.
- Magic is fiercely loving *you* better than anyone else could ever love you.
- Magic is following your bliss and wallowing in all the goodness and splendor you can imagine.
- Magic is having peace of mind, love in your heart, and a generous spirit.
- Magic is deeply forgiving yourself and choosing to love and be loved again.
- Magic is being comfortable in your own skin and appreciating every magnificent part of you.
- Magic is thinking positive thoughts and showing up in the world with optimism.
- Magic is curiosity, creativity, and answering the calling for your life.

Magic is unlimited! There are so many ways to create magic in your life in your own unique way. Please stop trying to duplicate someone else's life. You'll never live their dreams. You'll never walk their path. You'll never carry out their purpose, and you'll never arrive at their destination. Embrace the awesomeness of your originality, manifest your own dreams, confidently walk your own path, and live out your special destiny that's designed just for you!

Prune and Protect: Prune your life every day. If people are not adding to your life, they are subtracting from it. Don't forget that Becky is a Rose. She may not clip her thorns, so you will need to limit your contact with her. Protecting your magic is everything, so let me remind you of **this** gem from Chapter 5 again…

DON'T WASTE YOUR MAGIC!
- By *magic*, I mean don't allow these damn Beckys to take you off your game, to consume your spirit, or to snatch your joy.
- By *magic*, I mean the stride in your step, the sparkle in your eye, and the power in which you move around in the world.

- By *magic*, I mean your genius, the brilliance in your melanin, and the magnificence of your being.
- By *magic*, I mean your ingenuity, your divinity, and your integrity.

> "You *are* magic in all of your gigantic gloriousness! But you are not just magical. You are real, too, my Sister: a real human being with feelings that matter. You matter so much that you must make YOU the number one priority, so that you not **only** survive, but THRIVE within white society."
> – Catrice M. Jackson

Sister… you're not here to be miserable or mediocre. Your existence is significant. You have everything you need to win when Becky inevitably comes for you. You are greatness and you're here for a very special reason. I hope you choose to let nothing, *especially* Becky, stop you from being *all* you are destined to be. Go forth, my friend, and WIN every damn day!

Cracking the Becky Code Clues

There's so much more I want to share with you, but I'll leave you with these final tips.

Becky will be Becky no matter how far along in her anti-racism journey she is.

Don't be fooled by the illusion of inclusion. Wherever there are white women, there is racism.

You don't owe white women anything. You don't owe them your time or your energy.

Don't let Becky take advantage of your kindness. You do not have to educate her about your racial experiences. That is *her* work to do.

You'll know how far along Becky is on her anti-racism journey by what she says, how she behaves, and how you feel in her presence. Your intuition won't lead you astray. Pay attention to your gut feelings.

You do not have to forgive Becky for her violence, whether it is intentional or unintentional.

Becky is toxic and exhausting. Always put yourself first and protect your energy.

You do not have to talk nicely to Becky about the racism you experience. Call a thing a thing and hold her accountable for her violence.

You do not need permission or approval from Becky to be unapologetically you. Stop waiting and asking for it.

Stop serving Becky! You do not have to take care of her. She is responsible for her own feelings and behaviors.

When you are in the presence of Beckys, claim your space, own it, and do not shrink to make Becky comfortable.

Do not let Becky silence you. Speak your truth even when you are afraid.

Lay down the weapons you're using against your black and brown sisters. They need you and you need them.

Nourish, support, and amplify your black and brown sisters to help them sustain their magic.

Protect your MAGIC. It's your life source and you need it to thrive.
Go forth and WIN, my Sister! You are magnificent. You are glorious!

And amplify your JOY…

EVERY. DAMN. DAY!

Don't Waste Your Magic: How will you win every damn day?

_____

_____

_____

_____

_____

_____

_____

_____

_____

_____

_____

_____

_____

_____

_____

Afterword

"Believe in yourself. Believe in your greatness. Go out and make magic happen." – Catrice M. Jackson

Dear Sister,

Becky and her Beckyism will emotionally destroy you if you're not careful. Even when you think you are not letting Becky invade your life source (your joy), the Beckery will slither in like a thief in the night and steal your joy. Hell, Becky still gets under my skin sometimes, but now that I've decoded her and given language to her violence, I WIN more often. Beyond how to deal with Becky and her Beckery, I wrote this book to be balm for your soul and inspiration for your spirit.

Racism is a deadly virus. And Beckyism (White Woman Violence) is detrimental to your physical, emotional, and mental health. Just think about how much of your precious time and energy you've given to Becky and her Beckery, time you'll never get back. You could have been using that wasted energy on more fulfilling activities. Instead, Beckyism has been wreaking havoc in your life like the flu you can't get rid of. Becky has been draining your energy, exhausting you, creating anxiety and stress and stealing life from you. It's time to stop being sick and tired of Becky, literally. Remember, one of the intentions of Becky's Beckyism is to infect you with racism and destroy you. You cannot let that happen. You must WIN.

Becky is also playing a strong and strategic game of divide and conquer. One of the main tactics of white supremacy and whiteness is to infect people of color with internalized racism and oppression. Once you begin to consciously or unconsciously believe that whiteness is superior in any way, you abandon your own greatness, minimize the gloriousness in your fellow sisters of color and infect them with internalized racism. This false and fatal belief that whiteness is better is at the root of interracial conflicts. Don't consume this poison; it will kill you! Don't believe the stereotypes about your sisters. This is how Becky and Brad win! They divide and conquer! There's something extraordinary about your melanin magic! Don't you ever doubt it or forget it. I agree with what Jessie Williams says: "Just because we are magic, does not mean we're not real." Please do not take Becky and her Beckery lightly. Beckyism is racism, and racism will steal your life. You matter. You are significant. I hope you remember your purpose. And I say *remember* because it's not something you find, it's within you. You were born with a purpose, but life's challenges have caused you to forget why you're truly here. I hope you ignite your greatness, activate radical belief in yourself, and daringly live out your destiny!

Sister-friend, I hope you say "Nah, not today, Becky" every single day and refuse to be stirred into the Sunken Place. You have multi-dimensional magic within you! It's time. It's time to unshackle your undeniable greatness. It's time to unleash your significance. It's time to audaciously be all that you are destined to be. There's no more time to waste. You don't need Becky's permission or approval to be great or to do your damn thing. Suit up. Arm yourself with your Weapons for Winning. Go forth, Sister! And never waste your magic on Becky!

Types of Beckys

Super Becky: A savior-complex Becky who is notorious for jumping into conversations about racism to Save-A-Black or Brown woman without their consent.

Begging Becky: A performative Becky who is always sniffing around, panting for pats on the back, and begging for Ally Cookies (accolades and praise).

Wanna-Be-Black Becky: A Becky who loves to date black men/women, fetishizes black women, and appropriates AAVE to appear "woke."

Talk-Too-Damn-Much Becky: A talkative, centering Becky who adds no value, validity, or validation in race talks.

Know-It-All Becky: A condescending, apathetic Becky who intellectualizes racism by using a cognitive approach to understanding and discussing racism.

Love-and-Light Becky: An oblivious Becky who selfishly uses a sprinkling of love, light, and woo-woo talk to avoid facing her racism and to minimize your oppression.

Whining-Ass Becky: The most fragile Becky of all. She's perpetually hurt about anything and everything related to racism. She's a master at crying a river of White Tears.

Ole-Thieving-Ass Becky: A Becky who rapes and robs the culture of black and brown people to create an identity so she can feel alive inside.

Get-On-Your-Nerves Becky: A Becky who just gets on your nerves. She's a combination of Talk-Too-Damn-Much Becky and Know-It-All Becky, and she will exhaust the hell out of you.

Coworker Becky: A Becky who smiles in your face and tries to sabotage your success at work.

BWAM (But What About Me?) Becky: A Becky whose favorite Weapon of Whiteness is Centering. She becomes fragile and defensive when she's not getting all of the attention.

Weapons of Whiteness

White toxic feminism is full of *Weapons of Whiteness:* conscious and unconscious behaviors and words lethally used to deny your existence, stifle your spirit, silence your voice, and paralyze your progress. White women learn and acquire this assaultive arsenal of weapons, which is directly and vicariously taught and passed on by white mothers, grandmothers, sisters, and aunts. White women have been recklessly and unapologetically discharging these weapons against black and brown women for centuries. In the table, I list the top twenty-one weapons and give a brief description.

Weapon of Whiteness Racism = White Supremacy	Catriceology Definition
1. White Silence	When white women hide behind their White Privilege to refuse to speak up about racism.
2. White Fragility	When white women are unable to engage in real conversations about racism without becoming emotionally discombobulated, lashing out, and/or withdrawing.
3. White Innocence	When white women hide behind their White Privilege to avoid having to acknowledge, understand, and/or be knowledgeable about racism and its effects.

4. White Denial	When white women refuse to admit their own racism and/or acknowledge the systemic, structural racism and oppression of white supremacy.
5. White Entitlement or Centering	When white women consume time, space, and conversations; in other words, when they make themselves the center of attention. Also, when they expect to be taught, considered, and forgiven.
6. White Tears	When white women cry during discussions about racism, or when they express that they feel attacked, shamed, and/or hurt when their racism is pointed out or confronted.
7. White Superiority/Authority	When white women use their whiteness to dominate women of color: speaking for and over, interrupting, taking up space, cutting in line, and dismissing their presence.
8. White Derailment	When during conversations about race and racism, white women shift the focus, insert a different topic, and/or minimize, justify, and/or rationalize racism.
9. Whitesplaining	When white women attempt to educate black and brown women on racism, oppression, and white supremacy.

10. White Spirit-splaining	When white women use New Age and spiritual theories, concepts, and language to dismiss, minimize, and derail conversations about racism.
11. White Guilt and Shame	When white women become consumed and paralyzed by guilt and shame, and then project it onto black and brown women by shifting the blame.
12. White Collusion	When white women willingly and/or unknowingly co-conspire with white supremacy and racism at the expense of black and brown people.
13. White Saviorism	When white women demonstrate performative allyship behavior for the sake of being seen as the heroes and/or as showing pity.
14. White Gaslighting	When white women are abusers who silence, scare, and emotionally paralyze their victims. Gaslighting is a highly manipulative and violent act.
15. White Tone Policing or Dominance	When white women tell black and brown women how and when to speak about racism, oppression, and white supremacy.

16. White Righteousness	When white women judge people of color based on what is "white right," and demand right or wrong responses from POC through the use of White Interrogation. These kinds of folks are more interested in being right (perfectionist) in their Allyship than being effective.
17. White Interrogation	When white women ask black and brown people too many emotionally laborious DAMN questions and expect answers.
18. White Feminism	When white women claim they support and advocate for ALL women, yet fail to (or refuse to) center, prioritize, and amplify women of color and their needs and challenges.
19. White Privilege	When white women have the luxury of not having to think about, talk about, or experience racism. It is the unearned safety, access, permission, credibility, inclusion, preference, approval, and protection they possess only because they were born white.
20. White Performative Apology	When white women have been called out, called forward, called in, and/or critiqued on the use of a Weapon of Whiteness, and then they publicly apologize to look good, yet withdraw or lash out behind the scenes.

21. White Intellectualizing	When white women fail to express empathy for the racism black and brown people experience, and instead respond from a cognitive and intellectual space.

Weapons for Winning and Amplifying Your Joy

DARE to Speak: When white women DENY your truth, stories, and experiences, DARE to speak and call them out on their violations and violence. Of course, you must DISCERN whether this is a battle you're willing to engage in or not. If you decide that it isn't, remember that your silence will not protect you. If you fail to address Becky's violence, she is likely to violate you again. Iyanla Vanzant says, *"We must call a thing a thing."* This means you must identify and name racism for what it is by calling it out explicitly as white supremacy.

DISOBEY the Expectations: When white women DEFEND their racism, they *expect* you to stay silent and to accept their manipulative, defensive rationale. They *expect* you to understand their "mistake." They *expect* you to talk nicely to them about your pain while they cause it. They *expect* you to pull them to the side and not call them out publicly. They *expect* you to NOT shame them. They *expect* you to forgive them for their violence. They *expect* you to watch your tone and to not be angry. They *expect* you to explain or teach them about racism. DISOBEY ALL OF THOSE EXPECTATIONS!

DO NOT let them take your kindness for weakness.

DO NOT subdue your tone and your voice. Remember what Zora says: *"If you are silent about your pain, they will kill you and say you enjoyed it."*

DO NOT feel the need to talk privately about their racism. They will abuse you behind closed doors.

DO NOT let them manipulate you with declarations of shame and their White Tears.

You DO NOT have to forgive their violence.

DO NOT waste your magic and emotional energy on educating them. Be angry and mad if you want to. You DO NOT need anyone's permission or approval to express your anger. (Don't stay angry, however, because doing so hurts only you).

DO NOT FOLLOW THEIR RULES OF ENGAGEMENT. DISOBEY EVERY DAMN TIME! For centuries, white folks have had the expectation that black and brown folks would follow their white rules and expectations. You don't have to!

DISCONTINUE the Dialogue: When white women try to DERAIL the conversation about racism, know that this is an intentional tactic used to avoid looking at their own racism. White folks get extremely uncomfortable when talking about racism, and they will try to create an intellectual and emotional distraction to avoid dealing with their passive or active role in racism and white supremacy. Instead of following them into the violent white abyss, call out their attempt to derail the conversation. At this point, Becky has made it clear that she does not want to hear your truth or to stop her racial violence. DETACH. It's time to DISCONTINUE dialoguing with her. This is not a battle you want to try to win. It's at this point that we give away our precious energy and power to antagonistic white women who do not want to change. Walk away. You do not have to prove your humanity to them. They are NOT worth the agony.

DETOX and Delight: When white women try to DESTROY your joy, say, "*Nah, not today, Becky!*" On some days, it is worth the fight to go into battle with Becky. But I want to encourage you to choose a different, more nourishing option instead on most days. When the need arises, then dare to speak, disobey the expectations, discontinue the dialogue, and demand to be heard and respected. And don't forget to maintain your magic by detoxing yourself from the Beckyism. You are here for a very special reason and a divine purpose. Don't let Becky hijack your destiny! Taking care of yourself and making YOU priority number one is essential.

Resources

Tools for Your Journey

Recommended Books

Shifting: The Double Lives of Black Women in America
By: Charisse Jones and Kumea Shorter-Gooden, Ph.D

White Spaces Missing Faces:
Why Women of Color Don't Trust White Women
By: Catrice M. Jackson

Colonize This! Young Women of Color on Today's Feminism
By: Daisy Hernandez and Bushra Rehman

Unleash Your Significance: Active the Audacity to
Be All You Are Destined to Be
By: Catrice M. Jackson

Healing Spaces and Workshops

The BECKY Chronicles: Cracking the Becky Code Tour
An informative and empowering workshop for black and brown women to
learn how to deal with Becky, defy the Beckery, and amplify your JOY!

WETalks: Healing and Restorative Conversations About Racism
for Women of Color

WEWell: A Sanctuary for My Sisters Soul
A nourishing and supportive group for women of color.

Learn more about these offerings at www.thebeckycode.com

About the Author

Catrice M. Jackson, MS, LMHP, LPC

Catrice M. Jackson, is the Global Visionary Leader of the Awakened Conscious Shift, the CEO of Catriceology Enterprises, an international speaker, and a best-selling author. Catrice is passionate about empowering people and making an impact in the world. She's a humanist and activist dedicated to social and racial justice, because without either, people cannot fully or rightfully thrive in life. As an educator, consultant, and speaker, Catrice blends psychology, social consciousness, racial justice, and leadership wisdom into meaningful messages that propel people into action. Catrice is a dynamic difference maker with a voice that's unflinching, authentic, and powerful.

For as long as I can remember, I've always had something to say. I'm often compelled to speak up for the underdog and about the injustices in the world. I have a passion for raising difficult topics and engaging in courageous conversations, conversations that challenge "the way things are" and help transform lives. I value truth, freedom, authenticity, courage, and peace, and I intentionally infuse my core values into every human engagement, keynote speech, training, and workshop, and on any platform for which I am called to be a voice.

Empowering the lives of people is my passion. I'm on a relentless mission to make a difference, to do work that is meaningful, and to inspire others to use their gifts for social change. I believe justice is love in action, and I'm committed to loving on humanity by being an activist for racial justice. I'm here to challenge the status quo, to disrupt injustice everywhere, to dismantle systems of oppression, and to wake people up into an awakened, conscious way of being, living, and engaging.

Education

- PhD, Organizational Psychology, Walden University. (dissertation in progress.)
- MS, Human Services/Counseling, Bellevue University. GPA 3.97.
- Licensed Mental Health Practitioner (LMHP).
- Licensed Professional Counselor (LPC).
- BS, Criminal Justice Administration, Bellevue University. GPA 4.00 (dean's list).
- Licensed Practical Nurse, Western Iowa Technical Community College.
- Certified Domestic Abuse and Sexual Assault Advocate, Trainer, and Speaker.

Social Media Contact

Facebook: TheBeckyCode

Twitter: @Catriceology - @TheBeckyCode

Instagram: @Catriceology

YouTube: @Catriceology1

Websites: www.thebeckycode.com

www.shetalkswetalk.com

www.catriceology.com

Radio: SHETalksWETalk Radio – www.blogtalkradio.com/shetalkswetalk

Hire Catrice for Speaking and Education

Catrice is also available for speaking opportunities, radio and podcast segments, organizational training, anti-racism education, and consulting.

Contact Catrice: www.shetalkswetalk.com

Made in the USA
Monee, IL
22 August 2020